MICHAEL LANDERS

LEADERSHIP

BETWEEN THE

SHEETS

BOB BERK

Leadership Between the Sheets

www.leadershipbetweenthesheets.com

Edited by Gretta Hermes
Designed by Sean O'Connor

Printed in the United States.
First Edition
ISBN 978-0-9912477-0-7
Library of Congress Catalog Number 2014943431

TABLE OF
CONTENTS

FOREWORD
BY BOB BERK

Have you ever heard of or played the card game, "Between the Sheets"? It's also commonly known as "Acey Deucey" or "In-Between." It's a game of odds where your goal is to get a card that fits between the high card and low card that have been dealt to you. As cards are dealt around the table to all the players, the odds are constantly changing.

It's interesting for me to think back on a time when I was observing a game of "Between the Sheets." There was one person who was goaded into playing more hands than he should have, because the odds weren't in his favor. Another was a classic riverboat gambler who just liked to take risks. Then there was the person who always stayed within his betting discipline and typically came out the winner in the long run.

Leadership Between the Sheets reflects a similar strategy—it's about how we play this "game" called life. You are constantly making decisions that can materially change your life. At the same time, those decisions revolve around a set of core values and purposes that define who you are.

Living a fulfilled and significant life is a worthy goal. However, the way you live it, the way your children live it, and the way your grandchildren live it is going to be different. This book is about how you define your life, how others define theirs, and how allowing those differences can bring you closer, rather than pushing you apart.

As the anthropologist Don Schmincke explained, beliefs drive behavior and behavior drives results. You have to start with your belief system before you start to adjust behaviors and attempt to get different results.

What are your core beliefs? ...I encourage you to stay with them and at the same time, stay open-minded to the approaches and concepts I'm about to share.

This book is also about *choices*. Choices about careers and partners...and many more of the choices you have to make during your life. And, as Steve Job's said during his commencement address at Stanford, "You can't connect the dots looking forward; you can only connect them looking backwards." I chose the title, *Leadership Between the Sheets*, because it's about the most intimate decisions we make. I've made questionable choices, choices made from fear, and one really great choice—I asked Carole to marry me. My one-time business partner, Jerry Milgram, told me that he offered me a partnership at Milgram Kagan based on my ability to make good judgments, *after* I told him that I proposed to Carole.

I wrote this book because Carole taught me that the only way to intimacy is through vulnerability, and my becoming vulnerable and "real" has allowed me to experience real joy. I have learned that it's okay to be joyful, to live in gratitude, and to forgive. The key is finding joy in where I am today while still wanting more, and refusing to live in the gap between those two places.

Carole first challenged us to "grow" in our twenties, and then my big break-through came in my early fifties. That is another reason that I wrote this book. I want people to know what's possible and hear the lessons that I learned on my road to joy, and I want them to learn them as young as possible. My life has been, and continues to be, richer because Carole has shared it with me. I owe to her my thanks, my love, and my life.

Carole and I have great kids (adults). Although they will always be our kids, they have matured into wonderful people and have found and married great spouses. It has been an incredible joy to watch them on their journeys and to be their dad. I have learned far more from them, than they from me. Jenny and Michael, I continue to give thanks for how lucky I am, and how proud I am, to be your father. You have added so much to my life. Andy and Colleen, I love you as my children and for bringing so much joy to Jenny and Michael.

I am also writing this for my five grandchildren: Mason, Logan, Brayden, Lucas, and Alexis, as well as all the grandchildren of the world. I have learned that there are many stages and types of love. The love I had and have for my grandparents, parents, brother, wife, kids, extended family, and friends is different in every case. Now, I am experiencing another type of love—the love and joy of grandchildren. I remember buying my son Michael his first batting glove and him sleeping with it that night. And, during the time this book was being written, I bought Mason his first golf glove, and he fell asleep in my lap, wearing his new glove. It's the same scene, thirty years later. I am also sitting at Logan's dance recitals as I did with Jenny and am watching Brayden ride his three-wheeler, as Michael did—how fast it all goes. And now, Lucas and Lexi are in the first stages of learning to walk, taking their first steps toward independence and experiencing many "firsts." Wow! What a journey.

For the last twelve years, I have been a Chair (Executive Coach) for Vistage International, the world's leading CEO organization.

I want to especially express gratitude to Phil Kambic, President and CEO of Riverside Medical Center, Kankakee, IL., Dave Schreiner, President and CEO of Katherine Shaw Bethea (KSB) Hospital, Dixon, IL., Marsha Serlin, Owner and Chairperson of United Scrap Metal, Cicero, IL., and David Cox, Midwest Regional Vice President of Henkels & McCoy, Blue Bell, PA. who have allowed and given me free rein to work with them and their leadership teams.

To Jeff Mariola, President of Digital Brand Works, Chicago, IL., Annie Sul- li-van, President of Team Sullivan, San Diego, CA., Dave Schreiner, KSB Hospital, Dixon, IL., Amber Residori, Associate Professor, Olivette Nazarene University, Kankakee, IL., Monika March, Regional Sales Manager, The Economist, Chicago, IL., Kristi Hughes, VP of Product Development, Vistage International, San Diego, CA., Emily Rogers, President of Emily Rogers, Consulting and Coaching, Lakeland, FL., and Glenn Horton, President of The Horton Group, Orland Park, IL., thank you for reading the first draft and giving me direct feedback. While writing this, I am currently on a plane heading west, with Carole, to celebrate our 40th wedding anniversary. Later this week, I turn 64 and Jenny turns 36 on the same day. Collectively, we'll celebrate turning 100. It's useful to look back; however, a friend once told me that there is a reason that cars have big front windows and small rearview mirrors. The future is ahead. So, Mason, Logan, Brayden, Lucas, and Alexis, I have had, and I am having, a great life. I plan on celebrating, laughing, and crying with you in the years to come. I pray that you (and everyone else reading) will take some lessons from this book so your lives can be filled with love, joy, fulfillment, and peace.

I love you all,

Bob Berk, (B, Dad, Pop Pop, Coach)

SET INGOALTIONS: [IN·GOHL·SHUHNS]

The night at Ditka's restaurant in Chicago before my son Michael's wedding stands out in a special way for me, both as a father and as a leadership coach. The transitions taking place in his life were coming to an end with his marriage to Colleen—his new family was now his family. Although my beautiful, creative, and intelligent firstborn, Jenny, had been married on an equally amazing evening, an interesting event took place this night that I would take forward with me into my coaching career.

There was a wonderful mix of people at the rehearsal dinner that night, ranging from kids I had coached in Little League to friends my son and Colleen had met during their high school, college, and young adult years. Michael and Colleen went to high school together, so many of their friends knew each other. Close friends of Carole and I were also present, ranging from people we had met in grade school to wonderful new friends, and everyone in between. Adding to the fullness of the evening, one of Michael's friends, with the help of Jenny, Carole, and Colleen's family, had created a video, which captured and told the story of Michael's and Colleen's lives. This continuous flow of imagery, along with the fact that very few people needed to be introduced to each other, made the comfort and warmth of the night palpable.

At the beginning of the evening, Scott Rude, my son's lifelong friend, stood up to start the festivities as master of ceremonies. To my surprise, he started the toast by talking about Carole and me before moving to Michael and Colleen.

Upon rising from his chair, he turned to me and started the toast. "Mr. Berk, do you remember the best baseball team ever assembled—the first- and second-grade Flossmoor, Illinois, Little League Blue Jays?"

I said, "Yes, I remember, Scott."

He continued, "Do you remember our first day of practice?"

My curiosity piqued, I replied, "No. Where are you going here?"

Scott answered, "Well, I remember the first day. You sat us all in a circle and asked each of us what our goals were."

Laughing, I said, "Scott, I'm so sorry."

But he went on, "No, it was the first time anybody had ever asked me to set a goal. And I wouldn't be where I am today—a producer for the Golf Channel—had I not set goals."

Needless to say, the impact of that toast has remained with me over the years. Now, when I work with leaders, I ask, "Where do you want to go? How do you want to get there? What are your *ingoaltions*?"

You're probably wondering where the concept of *ingoaltion* [in•gohl•shuhn] comes from. I have been coaching CEOs for over twelve years, facilitated more than 600 meetings of executives and leadership teams, and conducted over 5,000 one-on-one coaching sessions with CEOs and C-suite executives. In addition, one of the projects that I have enjoyed most is leading a spouses group. This group came to life after I was challenged by the wife of one of my Vistage International members. Part of the mission of Vistage International is to "improve the efficiency and enhance the life of a CEO." The challenge was that the husbands (in this case, all the spouses were women) were in a growth and learning environment, and the wives were concerned that this might create a separation between them. So, together we planned and launched Vistage International Spouses Group. After one of the spouses asked what types of issues we would be addressing, I asked them all to take out a piece of paper and write down what issues they were interested in processing. Three common themes emerged:

1. My husband is a risk-taker, and at times, it scares me.
2. I am "mother of" and "wife of," but who am I?
3. I am living a life with more financial opportunity than my parents and siblings.

I was not surprised by the first two; however, the third one did take me back. Yet, as I think about the list—and as I discuss more fully later—we all define *risk* differently, and we are all seeking an identity, not a label that is placed on us. What happens when we live different lives than our parents or our siblings? How do we handle our children growing up and living different lives than we did? Fair isn't always equal! One thing I learned about "equal" in leading a spouses group is that a women's locker room is no different than a men's locker room.

So, as I sat down to create this introduction, I started thinking about leadership and the importance of goal setting, and how these qualities can differ between men and women. In a conversation I had recently with a young woman I coach, I revisited the spouses group I led and the concept of goal setting. After she commented on how women defined and approached goals differently than men do, I tossed out the concept of *intention*, wondering if it would be a more helpful word to get around any preconceived definition of goal. Realizing neither word actually got to the heart of what real goal setting is, it occurred to me what was really needed was a brand-new word: *ingoaltion*.

Cutting to the thick of what's holding you back from being successful in any realm of your life—whether it is your summer in Little League, your personal life, your career, or the world—it requires being aware of the filters through which you're looking at life and understanding what created those filters, whether it's your family, your environment, or any other story you live your life by.

So why not use the term *ingoaltion*? After all, an *ingoaltion* is merely a combination of goals and intentions. Before you scoff at my newly coined word, just take a moment to think about it. What have most of us done with our goals and intentions? We've turned them into dreaded self-limiting beliefs in rigidly defined boxes. However, sometimes just by renaming what is limiting us, we are better able to cope with it.

For those of you who don't like to use the term *goals*, what are your *intentions*? Are intentions a stumbling point for you? Then, what are your *ingoaltions*? Let go of your own interpretation of what it all means and try to redefine it.

What's your story? What happens to you when you don't make your goals or you don't fulfill your intentions?

First of all, you can't achieve all of your goals or fulfill all of your intentions unless you're fully awake.

What if you could achieve all of your goals *and* have that balance in life of family, spirituality, and other aspects you desire? From my perspective, that's a more joyous life.

I was "awakened" in my early fifties when I attended "Possibilities," a personal development seminar with professional coaching consultants Michelle Saul and James Newton, who shared the following analogy: In the early days of the television series *Star Trek*, Captain Kirk would be sitting up on the bridge of the starship *Enterprise*. Kirk would be looking out into space and he'd suddenly see that the *Enterprise* was about to get attacked by a warring clan called the Klingons. Kirk would call down to his chief engineer, Scotty, and Scotty would respond in his Irish voice, "Aye, Captain Kirk."

> " The greatest danger for most of us is not that our aim is too high and we miss it, but that our aim is too low and we make it. "

Captain Kirk would say, "Scotty, we need more power; the Klingons are coming. We need to get out of here."

Scotty would invariably reply, "I'm givin' her all she's got, Captain. I can't give you any more power. If I try to give you more power, we'd have to take the defense shields down."

What a wonderful metaphor that is! If you're busy defending yourself against your insecurities or thinking about how other people are judging you, how can you focus your energy on achieving your goals or intentions or be fully present with your kids or loved ones? However, when your defense shields are down and not being used, you can use all of your energy to be in the moment, to help you achieve your *ingoaltions*.

There is a Michelangelo quote that I live by: "The greatest danger for most of us is not that our aim is too high and we miss it, but that our aim is too low and we make it."

Personally, my goal (or I should say, my *ingoaltion*) is the same every year. It is, very simply, to be 100% in the moment 100% of the time, to be totally present with the person or the people I'm with—no noise, no chatter, just 100% present. The state I was in after having experienced the "Possibilities" seminar is what I continually strive to get back to, as it's the closest I can get to being awake all the time. And if I'm awake, then I will be able to be at my best and catch the nuances and nonverbal messages that people are giving off, so I can be the best I can be, whether I'm a Little League coach, executive mentor, father, husband, grandfather, or friend.

For many, business seminars, conferences, and other professional development experiences can be like a religious service. What do I mean by this?

Consider the following: how often do you take time from your busy schedule to reconnect with your community, faith, or spirituality? You may do this daily, weekly, or perhaps you only reconnect on significant holidays. You may spend this time with the best of intentions to follow through on the experiences and lessons you've learned; however, a few weeks later you are likely back on autopilot, living your life, not having put the new information or feelings you experienced to use.

A few years ago, one of my Vistage International groups was rafting on the Gauley River in West Virginia, and afterwards, we went into a local bar. Clearly, the music from *Deliverance* was playing in some of our heads. Yet, as I talked to some of the patrons at the bar, it became apparent to me that some were Ivy League grads spending time on the river before making long-term decisions about their lives, while others were engineers. One thing was certain, they were all from pretty good cross sections of society.

What do you think your initial thoughts would have been, walking into that local bar? How many of us immediately resort to judgment? How many of us take the time to shift out of autopilot and really learn each other's stories? And if we do, how long does it really stay with us? There is so much to learn when we stay curious.

As you read on, you will find that this book is a departure from the typical autopilot scenarios of leadership development. Instead, through rich, poignant stories that get to the heart of the matter—from my life, my family, my peers, as well as the people I have had the privilege of coaching—I will demonstrate that there is much more to being a successful leader in life than reading every leadership best seller and attending every seminar. Throughout the book, I will take powerful leadership concepts and provide practical thoughts, personal experiences, and proven steps to help you actualize these concepts into new ways to live a life with more success, more joy, and less stress.

In the pages of this book, I will help you cut through the "leadership clutter" and show you how you can make a positive difference in your organization and in your personal life. Regardless of your age, experience, generation, or life stage, what follows will rekindle your desire to be an inspiring leader and help you immediately apply what you have learned in your work and in your life. This is not just another business book. This is a *life* book.

So what is my experience? Where am I coming from? Why should you listen to me?

Like many of you, I didn't start out as an enlightened leader. The starting point for me goes back to when I was a young executive. At that point in my career, all I really wanted was for the people who worked for me to get to the same place that I did. What I ultimately realized in my "ah-ha moment," is that I was withholding certain information from them. More specifically, I was withholding information from them so I would be needed. Instead of sharing all of the information upfront, when my employees came into my office with a good

---

If they think we have all the answers, without worry or fears, what are we teaching them for when they have questions, worries, and fears?

---

idea, I would always add something, thinking that I was really adding value. Instead, they were walking away saying, "Why do I give anything to Bob? He's just going to change it anyway." I wasn't adding value, I was merely inspiring them to stop working because I would always have the better answer.

One day, I finally realized that the people who worked for me couldn't give me what I wanted if I wasn't giving them all the information they needed. I was sabotaging my ultimate goal, which was to get my people to do more of what I wanted them to do. It was at that point that I woke up, smiled at myself, and said, "This is ridiculous." I started opening up and giving them all the information. As Patrick Lencioni said in his book, *Getting Naked*, and as my wife Carole also told me, the only way to intimacy is through vulnerability.

As a boy, I often heard don't cry and don't show weakness. I was happy to hear a paradigm shift take place while talking with my grandson, Mason. We were sitting around the dining room table and Mason shared with me that he was scared of violent weather. I talked it through with him, reminding him how he was first scared to go into the water, to when he was comfortable going into the water as long as he was holding on to me, to graduating to wearing his "water-wings," to finally swimming, laughing, and jumping into the water on his own. Mason went on to say, "But Papa, you're not scared of anything!"

I responded to him, "Of course I am." It all comes back to the role of the leader. If they think we have all the answers, without worry or fears, what are we teaching them for when they have questions, worries, and fears?

From that point on, I tried to understand where I was holding myself back, and where others held themselves back. It's about people and self-limiting beliefs, why we self-sabotage, and why there's so much anxiety and stress. It's about why somebody who has two billion dollars and loses a billion dollars jumps off a building. What's that all about?

At one point or another, most people are confronted with their self-limiting beliefs, these stories which aren't true. It's how we filter and see the world through our experiences. As a child, I held the long-term belief that I wasn't good enough. As we'll delve more into later, it's a childhood story that I took well into my professional career and personal relationships—even nearly sabotaging my early relationship with my wife, Carole, through fears of being seen as a fraud. I finally realized that if I didn't stop withholding and go "all-in," I was never going to experience a full, loving relationship.

Ultimately, the people who are the real successes in the world are the people who are comfortable in their own skin. It's important to realize that, although you may love positive external attention and feedback from others, what's really meaningful is when those external goodies are the gift wrap. *The real gift is when you feel it yourself.*

So, what are your *ingoaltions* for being a better leader, friend, family member, or member of your community?

My *ingoaltion* is to put these different ideas in front of you and share my personal experiences so that they will resonate with you. In my current work, I am privileged to coach some of the most successful business people in Chicago, the United States, and the world. These owners and CEOs of small and midsize businesses are the ones that everyone was talking about during the presidential campaign of 2012—they are the job creators. Additionally, one of the real pleasures that I have had in life is coaching Little League baseball. What I have learned from these experiences is that what makes great Little League teams is what makes great family systems and great businesses. My teams always won. Yet, that was never the goal. As a matter of fact, my goal each year with my teams was to win one game and lose one game, so that the kids could learn how to do both. As I have learned from my friend, Dr. Rick Eigenbrod, a clinical psychologist with a focus on organizational behavior and leadership, growth is when you learn something new, and development is when you change as a person. And development usually happens after a loss.

I'm not afraid to make the invisible visible. I'm not afraid for people to be mad at me. In fact, I'm hoping that the book, in itself, does that. In many ways, I hope to be a mirror for people to say, "Hey, that's what I'm going through. I don't need to go through this alone." And along with that realization, the book will provide mechanisms to help get you through your challenges so that you can have more joy in your life.

As a dad, Carole has always reminded me, "if you're doing it for the kids, keep doing it, if you're doing it for yourself, be careful." And it is in this spirit that I am writing this book. My experience teaching a leadership seminar at one of the top-ranked schools in Illinois, the Walter Payton College Preparatory School in downtown Chicago has helped to put the frame around leadership in high school and college. As such, this book is also for high school kids, young adults in college, and my grandchildren—Mason, Logan, Brayden, Lucas, and Alexis—and for my next potential grandchild, or grandchildren, who I have not yet met, but I am already madly in love with. I plan on being here to share these stories, but just in case….

Doing things for others is way to grow in all aspects of your life. Great lessons can be learned in becoming a servant leader, a leader who is focused on getting their organization and the people in it what they need, at any level, and at any point in life.

Businesses that focus on its stakeholders and families that focus on their members really need to make it a priority to help them get there, so that they not only function better but also with more joy. Instead of focusing on themselves, they get the best results by truly helping others and being servant leaders.

I once worked with a client who was frustrated because an employee she valued wanted to do graphic design one hundred percent of his time instead of splitting it fifty-fifty with graphic design and project management work. My response was, "You need to figure out how to make it work that your employee is able to do graphic design one hundred percent of the week." In order to be a servant leader, you need to get your employees what they need. My client said, "Bob, you don't understand, we only have twenty hours of graphic design work here," and I responded "Exactly, if that's not here, you still need to help him find it."

The best teams work really hard and really smart, attaching themselves to a goal bigger than themselves, and they don't take themselves too seriously. As a case in point, I received a Father's Day card from my son Michael, during his senior year in high school. On the front it read, "Dad, you were my football coach, my basketball coach, and my baseball coach." Inside it read, "Don't blame me if I don't get a scholarship!" And for those non-sports folks who might come across this book, I learned the same lessons from my daughter Jennifer's choir and theater experiences. Although, I wish I had learned those lessons earlier.

I can't help but wonder, if I had been hit upside the head with these real-izations when I was twenty years old instead of fifty, how much more valuable would my life have been to me, my family, and those people that I chose to bring into my community? If I can help my grandchildren and all the grand-children of the world "get hit in the head sooner," it will be an honor and a privilege and the crowning reward of my coaching career.

For now, I am challenging you to STOP! Take a walk and give the following questions some thorough thought:

- Are you on a path to the life you want to live?
- Do you have joy in your life?
- Are you living a life of significance?
- Are you living a life in alignment with who you are?
- Are you living somebody else's life?

If you're not scoring yourself really high on all of these questions, read on.

If you scored yourself really high on all of these questions and don't think you need to read this book, I would suggest that you might want to ask your spouse, your kids, or somebody on your team how you rate…and then read on.

CHAPTER ONE
GET IN

At Vistage International we like to say, "CEOs sign up, but human beings show up." Through this, I've come to realize that being truly authentic and effective really comes down to a couple of overarching concepts—*ingoaltions*, as defined earlier, and *passion*.

Now that we are "working" together, I would ask you: What are your *ingoaltions*? Where do you want to go? How do you want to get there? Before we dig in, take a moment to really consider what these answers are for you and write your thoughts down. …Seriously. Write them down.

As we delve deeper into the concepts, experiences, and practical tools contained within this book, my hope is that you will gain clarity and focus around your own ingoaltions and passions—what they are, where you want to go with them, and how you want to get there. The question is *what do you really want*?

I have always had a strong passion for leadership, studying and discovering what makes great leaders tick. Although I never finished college, I did start down that path as a political science major. I've always been enamored by political science, both personally and professionally.

When my daughter Jenny was at school at Syracuse University, she would call me and we'd watch the television show *The West Wing* together. Based on this common interest and shared experience, Jenny and I strengthened our relationship while she was in college. Do you have those common interests, and do you share them with people in your professional life?

In his book, *Good to Great*, Jim Collins talks about our innate need to have a big, "*audacious*" goal—something to strive for, something that's bigger than all of us. John F. Kennedy did this on May 25, 1961 when he announced before a special joint session of Congress the dramatic and ambitious goal of sending an American safely to the Moon before the end of the decade. John F. Kennedy, as the President of the United States, probably had no idea how to accomplish this. But he had a vision; he had a big, *audacious* goal. By setting that goal, people who had worked in the private sector were now willing to work in the government for less money and put in more time because they were part of something bigger than themselves—sending somebody to the moon and bringing them back safely to Earth. This goal was achieved when *Apollo 11* commander Neil Armstrong stepped off the *Lunar Module's* ladder and onto the Moon's surface and ultimately, returned safely to Earth. As Armstrong said "that's one small step for man, one giant leap for mankind" – as he made the event bigger than himself.

Our country's history is replete with leadership at this higher level. When Dwight D. Eisenhower became the 34th President of the United States, he said we were going to connect the country with a system of state highways—again, something that he didn't know how to do, but he successfully set a vision for the country. In the 1930s, Franklin D. Roosevelt and his administration believed that if private enterprise couldn't supply electric power to every home in the United States, then it was the duty of the government to do so. The Roosevelt Administration saw its vision take foot in 1935 through establishment of the Rural Electric Administration (REA).

As a result of the big, audacious goals of effective, authentic leaders such as these, we are still enjoying the dividends of space exploration, interstate highways, the REA, and the commerce they created.

Don Schmincke, an anthropologist and co-author of *High Altitude Leadership*, conducted an unconventional study of trekking in the Himalayas that further explored this concept of goals. What he found is that on practically every trek—from ground zero, to ten thousand feet, and back to ground zero—the groups almost always stayed together until the end when they accomplished their last climb. However, on their way back to their base camp, after the last downward leg of the trek, all of a sudden, the discipline and structure broke down. Why did this happen? They no longer had a *compelling saga* or a *big, audacious goal* to go after and achieve. As a result of this lack, groups break down culturally and organizationally. This breakdown happens all the time in society and in business.

During my daughter Jenny's senior year in high school, the school won the 6A State Football Championship. John Wrenn, who was the coach of that team at the time, shared with me that almost every one of the seniors on that team was late in getting their applications into colleges. Reflecting back on this fact, had they achieved their goal? Were they thinking that there was nothing better ahead for them? If so, what they needed to do was to establish new, bigger goals!

That's a large part of why kids have senioritis. For twelve years of school we tell them, "Work hard to get into the college of your choice!" Then, when they're accepted and they don't have another goal set out, the effort and discipline applied to excelling at school breaks down.

You can also see this effect when people are nearing the end of their careers. What happens when people retire, when they don't have their next *compelling saga*?

Leadership, whether it is in business, your family, Little League, or trekking in the Himalayas, is tied to having a big, *audacious* goal, saga, or more collectively, compelling and inspiring *ingoaltions*. If you don't have a compelling saga for your team, they will create their own and it's usually not consistent with your vision.

It's also important to realize that anybody can be the catalyst for leadership and vision. Leadership doesn't have to come from the top down. It can, and often does, come from the bottom up. It all depends on the one person who is willing to step up and speak their truth.

Whether you consider the Arab Spring, the Tea Party, or the Occupy Movement, in today's world, one person with a cause can reach out and connect with other people. We've seen leaders arise throughout history in the most unlikely places. Rosa Parks, unwilling to sit in the back of the bus accelerated a generation of civil rights. Candice Lightner, whose 13-year-old daughter was killed by a drunk driver, started Mothers Against Drunk Driving (MADD), which grew from a small California grassroots organization into an international corporation with over 400 chapters worldwide.

I've spent a good portion of my life being a somewhat frustrated "employee." What I mean by this is that I've never been part of a committee where I ultimately didn't become chairperson, and similarly, I was never part of a sports team where I didn't become captain. Some of us need to be and are natural leaders. As a natural leader, I'm always looking for new opportunities.

When I coached the Little League Royals, a.k.a. the '89 Royals, I taught the kids to field ground balls by holding ping pong paddles upside down. In order to field a ground ball with two paddles in their hands the player would have to place their body and hands into the right position. When we taught the kids to catch fly balls, I had them throw their mitts on the ground and I would use a tennis racket to hit tennis balls up in the air, for them to catch. This would help them learn to catch properly because you can't catch a tennis ball with one hand. And when we taught them to use two hands in in-field practice, I would toss eggs at

> Being a truly authentic, effective leader is the ability for people at any stage of life to take on a leadership role, look for new things, and *change the lives of others*. And this opportunity is open to all of us, whether you are a natural born leader or not.

them so they would learn to cradle things in their hands. In every instance, the goal of teaching was to make learning fun—making it experiential and bringing in creative ways to get the kids engaged while learning the necessary skills.

Being a truly authentic, effective leader is the ability for people at any stage of life to take on a leadership role, look for new things, and *change the lives of others*. And this opportunity is open to all of us, whether you are a natural born leader or not.

Who are the leaders who have inspired you in your life? Did they set high standards for you? Did they see things in you that you didn't see yourself? Were they so passionate that you could feel it? Were they holding themselves accountable and not allowing themselves to be victims?

WHAT IT TAKES TO BE A TRULY EFFECTIVE LEADER

One of my first leadership experiences in the Little League was when my son Michael would come to me and say, "Gee, Dad, I'd like you to draft this person for our team."

And I'd say to him, "Mike, he's probably the best athlete, but I'm not sure he'd be helpful to the team."

Mike would press further asking, "Why not?"

And I would continue explaining to him, "Because the kids tend to follow the leader of the group, and that person can be disruptive. So I think we're better off building a team unit that will grow in the same direction."

I followed that model throughout my Little League experience. Sometimes we had the best athletes, sometimes we didn't, but there wasn't a year we didn't win the regular season or championship. Having a team that works together and follows the *right leadership* is critical. The right group with the wrong leader will just blow up!

So, just what does it take to be an effective leader?

EFFECTIVE LEADERS CAN SEE AROUND THE CORNER.

In 2000, *The Wall Street Journal* ran an editorial that set out criteria on how you should select the next president. It had nothing to do personally with Mr. Gore or Mr. Bush. Instead, it suggested you should pick the person who you feel has the best ability to *see around the corner*.

Seeing around the corner is about more than being intelligent; it is about being innovative. Jerry Wexler, a man I worked for during my career and who was credited with building large parts of Michigan Avenue in Chicago, suggested that "people who understand markets make a living; people who anticipate markets make a fortune."

I have never forgotten these insights and believe to this day that an ability to see around the corner and a willingness to put a stake in the ground around your vision are integral to being an effective leader.

EFFECTIVE LEADERS KNOW WHEN CERTAIN THINGS NEED TO BE BROKEN, JUST NOT THE WRONG THINGS.

I have had the pleasure of working with Glenn Horton, the President of The Horton Group, for about eleven years. Glenn has built a highly successful business and is one of those people who effectively moved his business beyond the entrepreneurial stage into a company that was able to scale. It's my belief Glenn is one of those of people who could run a series of different businesses. One of the many things that I've learned from Glenn is, in order for a business to grow, a leader has to be comfortable with certain things being broken, just not the wrong things! Red Scott, the former chairman of Pier One, says it this way, "Do first things first and second things never."

In order to be an effective leader, know that certain things need to be broken, and instead of trying to fix them, challenge people to step up. Too many times a CEO will bring reference to something that's broken, and yet not urgent in that instant, and drive the organization's focus to that, instead of focusing on the important things.

During a visit to a company office, the president of the company and I walked into one of the areas of the office and noticed it was really warm. In that moment he made a big deal about how hot it was inside, bringing attention to the climate issue, instead of focusing on the actual important things he should be doing. In response, I briefly took him aside and asked, "If your workers are hot, are they empowered to call the repair man and get the air conditioning fixed? If so, why are you using your time to get involved in that?"

The biggest mistake we make as leaders or as parents is micromanaging the activities and behaviors of others instead of the results. An example from my life is that Jenny did better academically in college than she did in high school. When I asked her why that was the case, she said, "Because you weren't helping me!"

EFFECTIVE LEADERS ARE WILLING TO DISRUPT THE MODEL.

As a successful disruptor, Tim Jahnke, President and CEO of ELKAY, believes that everyone needs to be aware of the proper rate of change within with their own business. ELKAY owns a significant percent of the water fountain business worldwide and yet, is planning for the day when water fountains will be extinct and be replaced by water filling stations. ELKAY's ability to disrupt their own model will, without a doubt, determines their future success.

I love the concept that Thomas L. Friedman used in his book, *That Used to Be Us*, co-authored by Michael Mandelbaum. He introduced the concept of "OODA loop." OODA loop is the training methodology the U.S. Air Force uses, originally designed by one of its officers, John Boyd. As the concept goes, in a dog fight, if you are slower than your opponent "you die." If you are faster "you live." The loop is Observe, Orient, Decide, and Act. It poses the questions: What are you observing in your market and in your business? How do you have to orient yourself, your team, and your family to the new reality? Based on your orientation, what decisions do you have to make? What is your action plan? How do you prepare your kids for the jobs that will exist in the next decade, not the jobs that exist today?

In another example, a high-end contractor in the Midwest had always been a union shop. After the economic downturn, he was going to bid meetings that had previously only been open to unions and were now open to all. He needed to orient himself in what he was observing. He needed to determine if he should stay a union shop and go after a larger piece of a declining market or open a non-union business. It was imperative for him to decide what decisions to make in order to stay relevant. What would his action plan be? The only thing for certain was that it was not business as usual. He right-sized his business and in doing so, won a greater market share of a smaller market.

A good example of the OODA loop approach can also be observed with what took place with General Motors (GM). At one point, GM was making large-size vehicles because their factories were set up to manufacture vehicles of this size. They stopped paying attention to the fact that the market demand was for smaller, fuel-efficient options. This opened the door for Toyota to fulfill a growing need within the marketplace.

Jack Welch, former CEO of General Electric, stated it best, "I am convinced that if the rate of change inside an organization is less than the rate of change outside, the end is in sight." As an effective leader, your main focus and goal should be to make your business obsolete before the competition does. Are you willing to disrupt the model?

EFFECTIVE LEADERS UNDERSTAND THE VALUE OF MAKING MISTAKES.

One of the worst mistakes I made during my career in the shoe business took place when I shifted my experience from men's retail shoe business to open a group of women's shoe stores in Dallas. The life cycle of women's shoes was much shorter than men's. In the men's business, I could reorder well into the third and fourth quarters of the year. Applying the same ordering cycle to the women's stock, I was in Dallas ordering shoes past October and November. That first year, after ordering women's stock, the owner of the company came down to visit. He and I walked the sale wall and kept walking and walking. It was glaringly obvious that I had over stocked. I asked him why he didn't call and stop me from ordering. His response was that if he had called, then we wouldn't have been able to take that walk, and I wouldn't have been able to see it. That mistake probably cost the company well into the hundreds of thousands of dollars. Yet, at the end of that trip, I built a model for buying that was used as a template for the expansion of our business and was used as a model in the specialty retail business for years to come.

Along these lines, there's a famous story of a young man who was training at IBM, who soon after joining the company made a six-figure mistake. Dejected, he walked into his boss's office with his letter of resignation. To his surprise his boss said, "Hey, if I just spent $200,000 on your education, why would I fire you now?"

How many of us are willing to let our family, friends, co-workers, or employees make mistakes? And perhaps more importantly, are we willing to let ourselves make mistakes and own them?

EFFECTIVE LEADERS ARE VULNERABLE.

As I have indicated, I truly believe leadership starts in your personal life. As a father with a daughter of similar spirit, our relationship was not always easy. However, a material shift took place one day. I decided to take her out for lunch because I was struggling with something, and I asked her for some help. I believe this marked a pivotal change in our relationship. One of the stories we tell ourselves as adults is that we can't let our kids see us when we're struggling, but I think it's just the opposite. If I don't let my kids see my struggle, then when they have struggles later in their life, how are they going to frame that?

An attribute of a great leader is to be vulnerable and be able to say, "I don't know the answer to this. I'm not afraid to make the decision, but I've never been here before. I'm asking for your help." Instead, how many of us sabotage our success by trying to surround ourselves with people who are not as strong as we are, just to make ourselves feel better?

My daughter, Jenny, is a Vice President of Human Resources at Edelman, the largest privately-held public relations firms in the world. She shared with me that a 26-year-old employee mentors a senior executive in social media. How many of you have reverse mentoring programs where the employee is mentoring their boss because they have a greater skill set? Similarly, my five-year-old grandson, Mason, can navigate my iPad far better than I can. I am learning it as a foreign language whereas he is a "digital native."

When I was the Chairman of the Camp Committee at the Jewish Community Center (JCC) camps, we did a study on what the kids wanted. My interpretation of camp was that it was team sports: basketball, baseball, and football that were valued. To the contrary, we learned that kids today had plenty of those activities. What they wanted to experience at camp was rock climbing and other more extreme sports. The by-product of this shift in activities was that kids now came home from camp and became their parents' instructors. In this case, Michael was able to teach me rock climbing, while I was able to teach him baseball.

I try to live my life by the following edict: *If I'm clear on what I want to do, make the decision. If I'm uncertain, get more information.* The ability of a leader to be human, to not feel the need to command all the answers, and to surround themselves with people who are smarter than they are, is the real key.

EFFECTIVE LEADERS ARE RISK-TAKERS.

There is a wonderful graphic that I discovered by Dr. Orin Harari in California. The graphic is of approximately 40 people in suits hugging a tree, with one person standing out on a tree limb. The caption underneath it says, "In today's world, who's at greater risk?" That image had a profound impact on me and how I view risk. We tend to think that everybody sees the world the way we do, but understanding that people define risk differently is an important part of leadership.

"In today's world, who's at greater risk?"

Take for example, Virgil Ivan Grissom, better known as Gus Grissom, the second man launched into space as part of the United States manned space program. It is rumored that Grissom's heartbeat did not change as the rocket launched. If five able-bodied men had been able to get me on that rocket and strap me in, I am fairly certain that my chest would have hit the capsule wall. In stark contrast, my guess is that Gus Grissom viewed risk as "not going!"

When I was growing up in Long Island in the 50s and early 60s, we would go to the local drugstore and eat a hamburger and a milkshake at the food counter. At that time, the number one profit center at the Walgreens drugstore chain was their food service counters. At the point they were at the top of their game in food service, the then president, Charles R. Walgreen III, shared with his senior management team, "We're going to be out of the food service business in five years." At the time, the senior management team was hesitant to give up on their most profitable form of business. However, what he saw that the senior leadership team didn't see was an up-and-coming company called McDonald's and their more efficient delivery and distribution system. Because of his foresight and courage to take the risk of breaking apart the business status quo in order to move forward, Walgreens was able to continue to provide pharmaceutical items to the consumer while simultaneously repositioning their real estate strategy.

In another instance of cutting edge risk-taking, Don McNeill, president of *Digital Kitchen*, wanted to move his business from a production shop to a digital agency. Don was well aware that people inside of his organization might resist this shift. So, he created and became President of "Team Disrupt" inside his organization. Don felt that if he could let the people who were doing the traditional production business continue, while he moved the business into the new market, then people within the company would want to eventually drift over upon seeing this new line of success. Don's calculated risk and vision has led to *Digital Kitchen's* expansion and success with such clients as HBO, BMW, The Cosmopolitan Hotel in Las Vegas, Target, Levi's, Microsoft, Warner Bros., Nike, and PBS, to name a few.

It's this ability to see around the corner, disrupt your business, and take the risk needed to move your business forward at the right time that will truly make you an authentic, effective leader.

EFFECTIVE LEADERS PROVIDE A GREAT CULTURE.

Here is an example of a great business culture. A start-up recognized a hole in the market, in online retailing and protecting "show rooming." The founder wanted to build an environment that was inviting to young, creative talent.

As you approach the office, the first sign that you see on the front door is, "No vendors allowed unless you have chocolate chip cookies. We like chocolate cookies." The sign effectively clues people in to the culture they are stepping into. Once inside, the graphics on the wall, including pictures of the two founders, are done in an Andy Warhol style. Everywhere you turn, you see a consistent message of culture. If you are there at four o'clock and you walk upstairs, you will hear the latest music that one of the employees has chosen to play. Each employee has an opportunity to play their music for everyone and share why it's their favorite. Beyond that, there are foosball tables, ping pong tables, and beanbag chairs strewn about for when people gather to visit. The entire office reflects the energy that's created by the people who work there. It's an employee-driven culture.

By establishing Buy Happier energy throughout the company, that culture in turn gets communicated through to their customers. Their review scores on Amazon under "experience" rest at around 4.85. In essence, "work happier" has led to "Buy Happier!"

Are you this clear about the culture in your company? Even more importantly, are your employees?

EFFECTIVE LEADERS SURROUND THEMSELVES WITH PEOPLE "SMARTER" THAN THEY ARE.

Another key ingredient to being an authentic, effective leader is being "smart" enough to surround yourself with people who have skill sets that you don't have and who are, well, smarter than you!

When I first started my work as a Vistage International Chair, I had the opportunity to work with Stuart Friedman, President and Founder of Progressive Management Associates, Inc. (PMA). One of the services Stuart provides are Organization Analysis and Design (OAD™) surveys and workshops, which are structured around the OAD™ "free-choice" survey, developed by Michael J. Gray. This is a tool that has helped me to better understand who I am, as well as assist other CEOs and individuals to more effectively realize how they are hardwired, and where they need to adjust, compensate, or modify to reach their desired outcomes.

Like many of these exercises, when I get a business test which allows me to better understand who I am, the first thing I do is give it to my family. And so we all sat around the living room with a glass of wine and took the OAD™ survey. The survey measures seven major constructs—Assertiveness, Extroversion, Process, Detail Orientation, Versatility Level, Emotional

Control, and Creativity. One of the traits that the survey revealed for me is that I don't have any patience. Of course, my son Michael was quick to quip, "You paid how much to find out you have no patience?"

As it turns out, I'm also an outcome person. So, envision crossing a bridge. I want to get to the other side just as fast as I can. If I'm smart, I'm going to have a process person who's going to say, "Hold up a second. Can I check the supports and make sure they can support your weight?" Then my next question is going to be, "How long is it going to take?"

My wife Carole leads by rules. Carole's the person you want in your accounting department. As a rules person, she's going to stand at the beginning of the bridge until we find out how fast we're going and whether it's best to walk single file or side-by-side.

It's really important that each organization has the outcome person, the process person, and the rules person. Unfortunately, we tend to hire people most like us. To round out that team perfectly, you'd have somebody in each one of those quadrants, and you would defer to them at the right times.

As an effective leader, your role is to set the vision, make sure everybody's clear on that vision, assign the right "smart" people, and then, get out of their way.

EFFECTIVE LEADERS ALLOW FOR OPEN COMMUNICATION AT EVERY LEVEL.

The best culture will allow for open communication at every level within the organization.

There is a famous story about the Fairmount Hotel Bar in San Francisco, California, that speaks perfectly to the true nature of open communication. As the story goes, the Fairmont was in the process of putting in a new elevator shaft.

As engineers traversed in and out of the hotel with plans and hardhats, the doorman at the time became curious and asked, "What are you guys up to?"

The engineers explained, "Oh, well, we're going to need another elevator shaft."

Now even more curious, the doorman continued, "Where are you going to put it?"

"We're going to put it next to the other two."

"How long is that going to take?"

Much to the doorman's surprise, the engineers said, "About a year-and-a-half."

"You're going to inconvenience our guests for a year-and-a-half?" the doorman gasped.

"Well, that's how long the process is going to take."

"Are you going to lose any rooms?"

"We're going to have to lose a room on each floor."

A bit perplexed, the doorman restated, "So let me understand this. You're going to inconvenience our guests for a year-and-a-half, and we're going to lose the revenue of a room on every floor."

And now the engineers were getting frustrated. "Where would you put it?"

"I'd put it on the outside of the hotel."

And ultimately, that's just what they did, and the bar atop the Fairmount became the number one bar in San Francisco.

As a business leader in the shoe industry, if I was in the office, and we were over budget on our shoe buying, chances are we would communicate to the stores to stop buying. However, if I was out in the field, visiting stores, and I saw that we were missing the best-selling shoes in the best sizes, I'd write the order on the spot. My experience is, we make defensive decisions from the office, and we make aggressive decisions from the field. In order to be truly effective we need to get close to our customers or empower those who are closest.

If you have a mailroom in your organization, are you constantly challenging the person in the mailroom to come up with a more efficient system to sort and deliver the mail? Or, do you just keep doing it the way it's been done all along? Do you create the kind of culture that allows for those kinds of suggestions?

As Daniel Pink said in his book *Drive*, what people want at all levels of any organization is *purpose, mastery,* and *autonomy*. Think about bringing those three things into every aspect and every level of your life, whether it's in your family, social circles, or your organization.

So, the question is, are you willing to be open? Will you accept being challenged?

EFFECTIVE LEADERS ARE "ON STAGE" 24/7.

Becoming an effective leader, is more than just creating a mission, managing people, or developing a customer base. It's about delivering a vision for your organization, and living it both personally and professionally. From the time a leader walks into their home, gets into work, or engages on social media, they're on stage—24 hours day, 7 days a week.

I coach a young man who's excellent at arriving at the parking lot at work and knowing it's showtime. His body language changes and people can see and feel it. But then he told himself a story that he needed time when he got home to decompress. Hearing this, I said, "Wait a second. You can come to work and coach yourself in the parking lot on being on stage, but you need to go home, walk in the door, and decompress? What's that story about? Why can't you sit in the garage, and say to yourself in the same way, 'okay, it's show time,' and go inside to be there for your kids and spouse?" That small shift, he said, has been "life-changing."

We tell ourselves a story, and it becomes a self-limiting belief. You can do it in your business, but you can't do it in your personal life? It makes no sense, and yet, we start to believe it.

And so, you may be wondering when *don't* you have to be on stage? It's simple. You don't have to be on stage when you're alone in your car, alone in your office with the door closed, or alone in a room in your house. But when you are with other people—you're on. Specifically, I would hope you'd want to be there for your kids. As Carole repeatedly tells me, "kids learn what's caught, not what's taught." This being the case, what are you telling them?

When I worked at Milgram Kagan, I went into Marvin Kagan's office one day. I had something I needed to talk to him about, and he had a stack of legal documents on his desk. His glasses were down and he was deep at work. I said I needed to speak with him, and Marvin actually turned his chair facing me and asked me what I needed. I told him what I needed and he said, "I'm in the middle of something that's time-critical. Can I see you later today?" And I said, "Sure."

A couple of days later, I was working at home and Jenny came home from elementary school. She came bouncing into my office and said, "Dad, can I see you?"

And I said, "Hon, I'm in the middle of something."

She started to walk out the door, and I said, "Wait a second. Stop." I turned my chair towards her and said, "Honey, what did you want to tell me?"

"Daddy, I just want to tell you I got an A on my math test." I gave her a hug, and with that she went bouncing out. How dare I decide what I was doing was more important than what she was doing, without even finding out what she wanted to tell me.

So, again, do you have to be on stage 24/7? No—only when you're interacting with another human being!

ARE YOU A MANAGER, OR ARE YOU A LEADER?

There's a time in business for leadership and a time in business for management, just as there's a time in families for leadership and a time in families for management. As the Saga Leadership Institute has established, managers focus their efforts around creating order, seeking compliance, providing structure, controlling individuals, outcomes, and situations, eliminating risk, and supervising. In contrast, leaders focus their efforts on disrupting order, seeking commitment from those around them, providing vision and direction, motivating others, taking risks, and inspiring others. Unfortunately, those of us who are managers in business might need to be leaders at home. If you try to manage your family in an ever-changing home environment, it's likely you'll meet with resistance and perhaps, even failure. In rapidly changing environments and times, people (both employees and family members) need good leadership, because leadership, as I mentioned previously, is seeing around the corner.

Once effective leadership has put the vision in place and inspired others to action, the time arises for the management process to begin. For example, after President Kennedy effectively planted the seed that the United States was going to build a space program, the time for managing the different processes and systems came into play.

Taking this one step further, I like Warren Bennis and Burt Nanus' distinction between leadership and management. In their book, *Leaders: The Strategies for Taking Charge*, they stated it this way: *Leaders do the right things. Managers do things right.*

A dilemma can arise when an employee given an instruction, does what he or she has been told to do, when the "right" thing might be counter to that. What might have happened if the staff assembling the O-ring for the space shuttle *Challenger* spoke up, or if the team at Toyota had stuck to the original guiding principles at Toyota, that anyone could stop the assembly line, might a fatal design flaw been discovered?

As I've alluded to previously, leadership goes well beyond business. For instance, in a family unit, how do you lead? In order to be successful in any specific type of meeting, there needs to be a clear outcome and clear ownership. So, whether you're in a business or family meeting, it's important to identify the desired outcome and who takes ownership of each outcome or process.

For example, in our family, if we wanted to take a trip, we would sit the kids down and tell them, "You know what kids; we want to take a vacation. It's your mother's and my decision to make; however, we would like your input. The trip is going to be a driving trip no more than five hours from Chicago." In this way, we were clear on governance and clear on the outcome we were seeking. Without this clarity, Jenny would end up choosing a trip to France, Michael would pipe in he wanted to go to Florida, an argument would ensue, and no consensus would be reached.

Ultimately, if Carole and I couldn't decide and it had to do with the kids, she was the tiebreaker. If it had to do with anything financial, I was the tiebreaker. Fortunately, in our marriage we didn't have to use this process very often, but again, there was clear governance about how the decisions were made.

Applying that process to a business setting, if you sit down with your boss and say, "Here's the outcome I'd like, and in my view I own this decision," and if the boss agrees, you now know his or her input, and you still own the decision. If you're sitting with your boss and it's his decision, then your role is to give as much counsel as you can and then be clear that it's their decision.

The role of a leader changes as circumstances, people, and markets change. In general, when things are disrupted, then you need to step up and lead. Lead with creative thinking and a focus on continuing to do the right things and adapt where needed. If things are going really well and you have the wind behind your back, then it's time to step back and let the managers manage.

Leaders do the right things and managers do things right. There are roles for leaders and managers in every organization. Throughout this book, you will learn how to clarify when to apply leadership versus management further. Ultimately, adaptive leadership is about adjusting to changing markets. Effective leaders make sure the ladder is on the right wall, so that their team is climbing in the right direction with them.

EFFECTIVE LEADERS ARE CONTINUALLY OPEN TO CHANGE

When Carole and I got married, Carole was what society would classify as a "caretaker." She was brought up in a family environment where when "Dad was home," she and her sisters were expected to be quiet and behave themselves. And so, that's the woman who came into our relationship. A few years into our marriage, Carole starting saying, "This doesn't work for me," and that's when she went back to school and started to do her work. She knew, once she started her developmental work, she would become a different person. It was at this point that she looked me in the eye and said, "I love you and I hope it works, but it's going to be different when I come out the other side."

Through her own growth process, Carole taught me how to have the courage to make that change. Ultimately, her life was okay, and my life was okay, but she wanted something better and different for herself. And to risk our relationship at that time to start on that journey, challenged me as a person to do my own work, to change, and to think about the other roles in my life.

Over time, businesses, couples, environments, and people change. And it's really a leader's responsibility to be open and willing to go down a curve of growth and embrace change in order to reach a higher level.

Are you willing to take a dip in order to reach a higher level in business or your personal life? Have you fallen asleep in any of your relationships? If so, why? To the best of my knowledge, you only get one shot at this life. You might as well live it with joy and not be afraid of change and not live in fear—whether it's fear of change, fear of death, or fear of anything.

There are no guarantees in life except, I guess, death. Everything in life is a choice. And every minute of every day, we're all responsible for the choices we make. It's about holding yourself accountable.

At the beginning of this chapter, I asked you to think about and write down your ingoaltions. Are you thinking about these differently now? If so, where is it that you truly want to go and how do you want to get there? What does your path to becoming a truly authentic and effective leader look like?

CHAPTER TWO
FIND YOUR FIT

Starting my business career in retail, I learned early on that one of the single biggest challenges for me was growing my business from one store to two stores. Surprisingly, expanding from two stores to 200 stores was not as complex. The greatest challenge arose around the concept of *control*. Initially, I had the choice to be at the flagship store one hundred percent of the time; however, once the second store was opened I wasn't able to dedicate more than fifty percent of my time at any single store. I now knew I had to depend on others in order to keep both stores running smoothly.

As I evolved and matured in my business career, I came to realize some people never make that shift. Instead, it remains important for them to have their fingers in all aspects of the business. And for those people, it's very difficult for them to grow their business because at some point, in order to expand, you have to rely on and trust others' expertise and give them the opportunity to shine.

That said, one lesson I have learned is, don't hire someone that you didn't learn something about the job from, during the interview. Because, if they couldn't teach you something about the job, then you're going to be spending a lot of time *doing* their job instead of trusting them to do what they were hired for.

When it comes to relying on and trusting others' expertise, a similar process should be considered with regard to your family. When do you start trust-

LEADERSHIP BETWEEN THE SHEETS

ing your kids to make appropriate decisions? My guess is that, as parents, most of us hold on too long.

Leadership "development" is about growth and change. As a businessperson and as a leader, the first question I would ask is, "Do you want to grow?" If the answer is yes, why do you want to grow? And are you willing to change? What are you willing to let go of?

Some people are better off staying smaller where they can be the chief salesperson or the chief operating officer. At this level, they can manage the financials and all other aspects of their business. Many individuals can't let go

Stress is not external. Stress is internal.

and embrace the concept we discussed in the previous chapter that, "in order for a business to grow a leader has to be comfortable with some things being broken, just not the wrong things."

Are you at a stage in your leadership where you can accept some pieces being broken? Are you stifling your growth, your business's growth, your employee's growth, and maybe even some of your family member's growth by keeping things whole? Are you not allowing things to be broken?

THE THREE STAGES OF LEADERSHIP DEVELOPMENT

My experiences with leaders across the globe have led me to the realization that there are three levels to development and growth, both personally and professionally.

1. Level One: Being in Control
2. Level Two: Hire Stronger People
3. Level Three: Visionary Leadership

Level One: Being in Control leadership is where you decide to 'hang your own shingle,' or operate a business unit and move outside the realm of working for someone else. Ultimately, I praise people who have the courage to start an entrepreneurial business. This type of leadership also exists within separate silos in corporate structures.

It's interesting, how many conversations arise where an entrepreneur express-es that the professional manager has less stress because they're working with somebody else's money and the professional manager thinks the entrepreneur has less stress because they get to make all the calls and decisions. No matter which camp you're in, keep in mind the grass is not always greener on the other side, it just appears that way. As I will go into more depth later, stress is not exter-nal. Stress is internal.

To me, shifting from being a professional manager to being an entrepreneur has more to do with innate personality traits. Entrepreneurs typically don't work well for somebody else and might even not play well with others in the sandbox. It's often this innate drive and initial solo success of the entrepreneur that ultimately gets in their way of moving into stage two of leadership development. It is that they feel "safe" if they are controlling everything.

This level of development can also be seen in a personal sense. Once you enter into a relationship, get married or decide to start a family, it's important to be able to move outside the realm of your personal "solo success" and cohabitate with others.

Level Two: Hire Stronger People leadership is when your business gets more complex in its layers of management. This can be the stage when you start to build the business, hire levels of management and start to have distributors, or open a second store or other offices outside of your initial territory.

In my experience, when entrepreneurs experience stress within their workforce they often habitually shift back into doing the jobs they used to do. Interestingly, they desire a strong workforce; however, strong people don't want to be micromanaged. And therein lies the paradox. I have also experienced that A-people hire A-people because they are comfortable having smart people around them. Similarly, B-people tend to hire C-people who are typically okay being told what to do.

If you hire people who you can tell what to do and are who are going to do what you're telling them, chances are they're not as competent, which creates a dilemma. Conversely, if you have weaker people it's likely you want them to step up when they're not. If you hire stronger people, they're going to start taking some initiatives that might make you uncomfortable, and it's this discomfort, either way you choose, that will stop you from growing.

A similar situation can arise within families. As children mature, it's important to consider what decisions they can make. How can we slowly allow them to make more of their decisions?

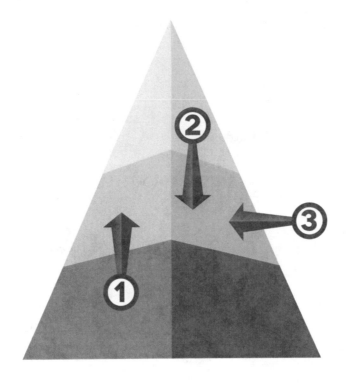

*If the CEO goes back in to fill that void and
do someone else's job, any forward momentum
or growth will come to a screeching halt.*

Glenn Horton, CEO of The Horton Group, pointed out the impact these levels have on organizational development using the triangle above.

At level one, everyone is at the bottom of the triangle, doing and enjoying everything. These individuals like being in the tactical weeds. At some point, an entrepreneurial CEO will want to reach a higher level and will move to the top of the triangle to move the company into new markets and develop new products or new ways of doing things. This creates a void and subsequently, new tensions within the organization. CEOs in this position generally like to think that the people at the bottom of the triangle will have the desire to move up as well, but historically, they don't. They would have moved on or challenged the organization if they wanted something different.

If the CEO goes back in to fill that void and do someone else's job, any forward momentum or growth will come to a screeching halt. At that point, the only option to restart growth is to bring someone else in from outside the organization, which in turn starts to affect the culture. If resistance within the organization stops the leader from moving the company forward, the organization will stop growing. As "new endeavors" take foot, new people need to be brought in to help change the culture, allowing the CEO to continue moving the company forward. At this point a conflict can develop between the new and old ways of doing things. Interestingly, if you look back at companies that have successfully shifted their culture, it usually takes place after they have changed *people*.

A few years ago, I was coaching a young man who was working in his father's company. He shared with me that his dad was continually telling him to step up within the company. However, when he did step up, he would find his father still in the same spot. And I asked him, "Is it possible that both things are true? Your dad does want you to step up, and your dad isn't quite ready to let go of control yet. The only way that's going to work is when you meet your dad in that spot. If you go back to your office, nothing's going to change. If you can say, 'Dad, I have this, go back to your office,' your behavior will change the relationship and enable the company to continue growing."

Don't get me wrong, asking an entrepreneur to let go and let you make those decisions is a difficult task. You can probably envision how difficult that is for a son. Can you imagine what that's like for a hired gun?

A large portion of my work in my Vistage International groups is just that. If you report to someone else, what's stopping you from saying, "I have this." or "I'll handle it?"

There was a study that looked at the Japanese "empowerment culture" as a business model when it was brought into the United States that helps explain the reasons this approach often breaks down. The concept of empowerment is driving decisions down as low in the organization as you possibly can. I feel the most efficient organizations are where people are doing the job above their current position. In 92 percent of companies that tried empowerment, it didn't work. So, a study was done on the eight percent where it was successful. What they found was, in those eight percent of the companies where empowerment worked, there was over-communication up to the CEO. If the leader needed to seek out the information, it didn't work. In these instances, they would focus on what was going wrong. The lesson here is to develop a culture where people are able to over-communicate up which takes a certain confidence, relationship, and trust.

When I was the Vice President of Merchandising at Milgram Kagan, I inherited a situation where the company was grossly over-inventoried in handbags, but severely under-inventoried in white, bone, straw, and canvas bags as we headed into the spring season. I went to the handbag buyer, and after having been fully apprised of the situation, I asked her how she wanted to proceed.

I sent her back to her office and I went to the Chief Financial Officer and asked, "What's the impact if we don't clean this up until fall?" Unsure as to the next steps that she wanted to take, we went to both of the owners of the company, for advice. Jerry advised us not to buy any bags, so as not to get further over-inventory. After speaking to Jerry, we then went to the other owner, Marvin, for his take on the situation. Marvin advised us to buy the new bags because missing the season wouldn't help the current over-inventory situation.

I sent Maureen back to her office and I went to the Chief Financial Officer and asked, "What's the impact if we don't clean this up until fall?"

He said, "We have the cash to do that."

So, I went back to her and asked, "Okay, you heard the two sides of the argument. Which way do you want to go?"

After pausing for a moment she said, "I think Marvin's right. We should buy the bags."

Trusting her decision, I said, "Put together a plan of how much you're going to spend." I then took the budget to the Chief Financial Officer and he verified we could cover it. I put together a plan that showed how we would get the inventory back into plan by late fall.

The most important step I took was what I did next. I went into Jerry's office and said to Jerry, "Your advice was to hold off on buying any additional inventory. So, I just want you to know, you're going to see a series of bags come in over the next six weeks, and here's my plan for getting the inventory back in line." I owned the decision and the key was my communication.

If you're going to empower people, instilling and enforcing "communication up" is the critical component.

Taking this back to your family, how do you get your children to communicate up so you don't have to go in and get the information? Think about it. If you ask your children to be home by twelve o'clock, "life" can happen. However, instead of coming home at twelve thirty, what if they over-communicate up and call at eleven. As a parent, you would then have a choice to either go and pick them up or allow them to arrive home after their curfew. Because of this level of communication, you now have options and an opportunity to empower your children.

Whether it's in business or in family life, many people don't understand why development into level two doesn't happen—the answer revolves around open and honest communication and trust.

Level Three: Visionary Leadership is the stage of leadership development where you can run an organization at any level. Leaders at this level have clearly defined measures and don't get caught up in the "how" with their team. They just get into the "why" and "what" and don't have to own the way that it's done.

As long as it fits the culture, ethics, and morals of your organization, let the people who own the responsibility make their decisions. How do you get out of those operations and trust? The only way to do that is to hire people who are actually better than you at "it," whatever "it" is. If you get into the "how" on the execution piece, then you will never be able to operate at the level of an authentic and effective leader. And how can you hold someone accountable, if you are the one making the decisions?

A few years ago, I was working with someone who was hiring her first assistant, and I asked her what she was working on. She responded that she was working on writing a job description. I suggested that she stop and take a different approach. Instead, I proposed she meet each of the candidates and let them write the job description. Shouldn't they know better than she what the optimal candidate for the job should look like? More importantly, how much time do you think would be wasted "trying to train" an assistant to be "the one"?

I was also working with a regional hospital that was bringing in their first outside, rather than promoted from within, vice president in twenty-two years. They were trying to develop what the first month would look like. I suggested they let the new vice president develop the plan, as she came from an organization that brought in senior level executives all the time. Why did they think they had to do it?

If you think about this organizationally, in the field of sports, if a head football coach doesn't trust his offensive coordinator, his defensive coordinator, or if he doesn't trust the special teams coordinator, there's going to be all kinds of dysfunction because the head coach will be compelled to do the job of the assistant. Instead of trusting that the game plan is correct, working on the strategy, and then trusting his team to execute it.

Conversely, CEOs are often tempted to step back in to be the person in charge, when they really shouldn't be. Peter Schutz exemplified how a Level Three Leader effectively operates. Although he as a CEO led the turnaround at Porsche, if he went into the pit where a team was working on a car and the head of the pit crew pointed at Peter Schutz and said, "Pick up that tire and bring it over here," Peter would have gladly done it. As he accurately saw it, the person who was running the pit was the person who was in charge.

In a different but still effective leadership style, at General Electric, Jack Welch *owned* leadership development. As such, he was an integral part of the company's curriculum and policy development. When visiting an office he would always ask, "Who is ready to take your place?" This important execution remained consistent within their company, contributing to their success.

When you consider flawless execution, whether it's in acquisition, customer service, distribution, marketing, or recruitment, what does your company need to execute flawlessly in order to successfully grow? For that matter, what does flawless execution to support your family's growth look like?

HOW ARE YOU HARDWIRED?

I have worked with a senior leadership team and their outstanding President and CEO for six years. At the time, he was integrating two vice presidents into his team of existing vice presidents and he wanted to make sure that the integration went well. After sitting in on a couple of meetings, I came to realize the issue wasn't integration. Rather, there was more of a trust issue and a silo issue inside the organization, between all of the vice presidents, new or existing.

Additionally, in observing the behavior inside the group, what I discovered was that the CEO loved to argue and it wasn't just for the sake of arguing. He'd challenge and present ideas, creating a lively "give and take" atmosphere, but one misconception of his was the fact that he thought it was a fair fight. It was clearly never a fair fight. And so my job became to try to make it a fair fight amongst the team.

What people eventually came to realize was that the CEO just liked to have rigorous debate. There was no baggage attached to these interactions. When it was over, it was over. He merely appreciated good strong feedback and good strong comments, and trust was eventually built around the fact that there are no reprisals.

We did an exercise set out in a *Harvard Business Review* article (January/February, 2011) entitled, "The CEO's Role in Business Model Reinvention" by Vijay Grovindarajan and Chris Trimble. I asked everyone what they felt their best characteristic was. Then, I asked them to evaluate each other. When the CEO shared that he felt his strongest characteristic was strategy, a fun and heated conversation ensued. As it turned out, he was the only one who thought that was true.

When the CEO tried to defend why he thought he was a strategist, one of his team members said, "No, that's just taking what we're already doing and replicating it in other markets. That's not strategy. That's execution." This was a real eye-opening moment for the CEO and the entire leadership team. And as a result of this exercise, he became more curious. He invited young leadership into strategic discussions and added a member to the senior team who was a good strategic thinker.

When you can have those kinds of honest open conversations about reality and put a mirror up to each other, no matter where you are in the organization, that's when organizations get real and set upon a path to real growth.

So, where do you fit in?

Going back to Jim Collin's *Good to Great* model, he talks about having a big hairy audacious goal and having the right people in the right seats on the bus. How many times have you hired the wrong person because you went to an immediate first impression that you liked them?

This is the reason I suggest my clients utilize assessment surveys. These surveys can help you move away from biases and preconceived notions, allowing you to get to know who people really are at their core.

There are many different tools out there that you can use to determine your and others' strengths and weaknesses, such as the DiSC® profile and Strength's Finder. However, the two surveys that I have had the best success with are the Emotional Intelligence (EQ) Assessment and the Analysis, and Design (OADTM) assessment tool.

I use Bob and Heather Anderson, from Stowe, Vermont to facilitate the EQ assessment to my groups. It's quite funny to watch my groups react and make their first impressions when Bob Anderson walks into the room. He lives in Stowe, but by his appearance and the way he talks and behaves you would think he's an Oregon tree hugger. In reality, Bob is an all-American athlete and Harvard graduate who enjoyed a successful career in the Special Forces. However, when he walks in with a big picture of his kids on his t-shirt, portraying himself as he does, people typically make the wrong assessment. He purposely overdoes the tree hugger bit as part of his theatrics in introducing the EQ assessment.

As I mentioned briefly in the previous chapter, I like to work with Stuart Friedman, president of Progressive Management Associates, Inc., when administering the OAD™ survey to my clients. Many of my clients rely on Stuart's work in their interview process, as well as when they are stuck on how to best coach one of their employees.

For example, a CEO that I was working with wasn't happy with the integration of a new Vice President of Sales and Marketing into her company. She was uncomfortable that he had not developed a sales training program. He even accused her of micromanaging. We pulled out his OAD™ and noticed that he scored very low in process. He could be very successful building his business, but chances were that he wouldn't be a good trainer or be able to develop a training program. The options were now apparent to the CEO — measure the results of the department and if you truly believe that the training is important part of the success, then someone else would have to own that piece.

I like to recommend individuals take an assessment survey such as the OAD™, E.Q., DiSC®, or Strength's Finder because I find that they provide you with invaluable insight into your "hardwiring"—a key component of your makeup that doesn't change. As Stuart likes to say, "It isn't about *what you do*. It's about *who you are* and what you do with it." It's about knowing yourself and knowing where you need to adjust, compensate, or modify, because "who" you are doesn't change. From that point, your personal growth comes down to how easy or difficult it will be to make any desired changes.

The good news is that there isn't a "preferred profile" for a CEO. When using any of your survey results, the crux of your development comes down to: knowing who you are, what you want to do, and where you want to go. And then, knowing the gaps between who you are and what it's going to take to get those things done creates real development.

I would suggest that you use the results of whatever survey you choose to more accurately assess what your natural tendencies are. From there, you can determine what modifications you may have to make in order to reach your desired level of leadership.

As a leader, I'm very assertive, extroverted, and have very low patience. So, the big trap for me in my career development was that I was always answering questions for everybody.

I never would have reached Level Two leadership had I not been made aware of my hardwiring, accepted feedback, and coached myself. As a matter of fact, in the early days when I managed multiple stores, I would frequently go into one of the stores, aggressively and with no patience, point out the things that needed to be fixed and leave. I had no awareness of the wake I was leaving behind me. As a result, a manager once, and rightfully so, handed me the keys and walked out. I can now look back on the incident and say, "Good for him!"

WHERE DO YOU FIT IN?

There is no "one way" to be successful. As leaders, we are who we are and the traits we have are the traits we have. Those aren't going to change. It's not a question of "are we at a certain level," it's about having certain traits and behaviors at a certain level. In other words, the person who has assertive traits is going to be a natural, *Level One: Being in Control* leader, and will work best at that starting level. As a *Level One* leader, you know what you want and you know how you want to set it up, you have an idea of how you see it, and in terms of driving the business, that's useful.

As you move up to *Level Two*, you now have to back off that command and control approach, to guide, manage, and mentor people. As a *Being in Control* person, that will be a challenge because of your natural tendencies. In order to grow, it will require stepping out of your natural profile, asserting yourself, and telling the people working for you exactly what you want and why you want it. This can be challenging because being open to others' ideas about how to do something doesn't naturally come to a *Level One* leader.

In order to grow, you have to look at your individual experiences. Your natural tendencies will indicate how you build relationships and rapport with the people around you.

WHAT'S HOLDING YOU BACK?

I had an interesting conversation with one of my friends who owned an insurance company and he said something that sort of riled me. He said, "I've really helped my group, my guys; I've made them a lot of money." In response I said, "Have you ever looked at it? Maybe they've made you a lot of money?" But he was unwilling to go there.

How often do you recognize and support the people who are helping your business grow? Couldn't the housekeeper in the hotel know more about the elevator lobbies than the general manager? Ben Peck at Wohl Shoe Company said, "Grow your people and then let them grow your company." That's what *Level Two* and *Level Three* leaders get that *Level One* leaders don't.

There was a wonderful exercise in the *Harvard Business Review* that I referenced earlier that suggested every business needs to have somebody who's responsible for executing the operations of the business. Somebody should be responsible for getting the company to stop doing things, and somebody should be responsible, and get paid for, making mistakes. My interpretation of that was if everyone in the organization was being paid for operational excellence, how would we stop legacy issues and how would we be innovative?

However, nobody was being paid to get us to stop doing things. How many companies are doing things just because of their legacy, instead of paying somebody to stop doing that?

When I first became President of Milgram Kagan, I asked my administrative assistant to stop sending out every report that was being sent to all the management in the organization. I instructed her, "Let's just wait a week and see what they miss." It became very apparent that a lot of the reports had been built a long time ago and that people weren't paying attention to them any longer.

Who's being paid, within your company, to stop *you* from doing things and ending some of the legacy procedures and methods that are not longer effective? Who's being paid to make mistakes? Most importantly, who's being paid to try new, different ideas, to move the company forward? Are you the roadblock?

Earlier I shared a story surrounding my daughter Jenny. When she was a teenager, I went to her with a problem that I wasn't quite sure how to handle, and I became vulnerable. This one instance changed our relationship for the better, forever. The exchange wasn't father to daughter. Instead, the conversation placed us on equal footing. Although I was the adult, that didn't mean she saw things my way, or that I had all the answers. This also freed my family up to know that later in life, they don't always need to have all the answers.

When it comes down to it, it's not about the answers, it's about the questions. When do you converse with your children as adults? When do you allow them to make choices?

Well, it's the same thing within a healthy organization. When do you allow your direct reports to make their own decisions?

Stop hiding behind thinking you have to have all the answers. The truth is you have to have the questions. That's how families and organizations can grow and prosper.

Leadership Between the Sheets is about achieving joy in every level of your life. Wouldn't it be helpful not to feel like you have to have the right answer all the time? Wouldn't it be joyful to watch your employees and children achieve things that maybe you were holding them back from? Wouldn't life be better if you weren't a victim of others' behaviors and instead owned, in a light-hearted way, your weaknesses and inadequacies? Wouldn't your partnership or marriage be better if you could laugh at the silliness of your beliefs and relish in your differences?

As Marshall Goldsmith said in the title of his book, "What got you here won't get you there." What do you have to let go of?

CHAPTER THREE
LIVE AWAKE

When I went to San Diego, California, for my first training as a Vistage International Chair, right before the 2000 presidential elections, my belief was that I was going out for a business training to better facilitate and lead groups of CEOs. To my surprise, the real message of the training turned out to be, "You better know who you are and what you are bringing into the room!" In working with CEOs and doing one-on-one coaching, it is really important to know what issues we, as individual chairs, are bringing into our member groups.

Now these were the same principles that my wife, Carole, had been trying to drill into my head for years, but in that context, I wasn't able to hear it. However, having it framed in business made me more open to accept this principle and really take it in. This blending of personal and business started to become more real to me, as I learned that leading business is just like everything in life—*it's about showing up 100% of the time in every single moment.* It's about truly playing, as I like to say, "all-in."

This two-week training program was a pretty deep dive for me. At the end of each day, I would call home to Carole and share some of what I had learned from the facilitator, James Newton, of Newton Learning. As you may have guessed, her exuberant response was, "I love this guy!" The reality was, he was framing things in a way that I could hear because it was related to business development, even though the crux of it was how to be genuine and understand what baggage we as human beings are bringing into our relationships.

How many times can we hear something like that from our spouses, significant others, or family members? I would venture to say not very often!

The most valuable lesson this training taught me as a Vistage International Chair, father, Little League coach—and as a person—was there are many different ways to connect with people. And so in my practice, I've always tried various approaches until what I was trying to impart became real to the person I was coaching. As we touched on earlier, it's about learning how people process information. Over the years, I've discovered there are three major types of people: outcome-driven, process-driven, and rules-driven. If you're an outcome person, you're not going to feel safe until we talk about possible outcomes, if you're a process person, you're not going to feel safe until you understand the process we're going to use to get there, and if you're a rules person, you're not going to understand or feel safe until you know the rules of engagement.

I have to remind myself when I'm speaking to a broad audience to always start with the outcome and then introduce the process and rules we're going to apply, so every type of communicator understands how we're playing. I've found that my most effective speaking engagements, coaching sessions, and group facilitations are when I have referred to these three channels of communication, while simultaneously weaving in my own experiences and lessons I've learned.

It's not unusual to think that we're having the same experience as everyone else. However, how many times have you experienced something only to discover that your experience was different from those of others? Do you communicate differently than them? Are you open to other people's modes of communication?

As we explore in more depth, there are many considerations to take into account in order to truly live life all in. Connecting, engaging, and communicating with people on a personal and professional level are just a few of the keys, albeit very important ones!

HOW DO YOU CONNECT, ENGAGE, AND COMMUNICATE?

Quite often people will say to me, "How do you remember what the speaker said? How do you grasp it? You're quoting verbatim from speakers you heard awhile ago." Well, it's because the noise is down and chatter is not going on in my head. I'm not thinking about what people are thinking about. *I'm listening, being 100% in the moment.* Or, as my kids point out, I might be making it up as I go!

The truth is, I've never been a detail-oriented person. By the time I'm done reading a book, I can't tell you a date, a character's name, or the name of a town. I probably can't tell you the title of the book or even the author for that matter! However, I'll always remember the concepts and the stories that get to the heart of the matter. That's what has really driven me into the work I've done in education.

Education, whether it is in leadership or the family unit, is really about understanding how the person learns, not trying to force him or her into a box; it's about taking the time to really try to understand how he or she functions and works.

I have never understood why we make people memorize by rote, instead of having them learn concepts. Certainly, there are some careers and practices where memorization is essential, but is this method the best way to create innovative, thoughtful leaders? Education, whether it is in leadership or the family unit, is really about understanding how the person learns, not trying to force him or her into a box; it's about taking the time to really try to understand how he or she functions and works.

We hear a lot of buzzwords regarding "living in the box" and "thinking outside the box." I heard it said best this way: "Don't think outside the box, get outside the box and think." The more we can expose ourselves to new ideas, try new things, and embrace new approaches, the more our world expands and the more we can truly live *100% in the moment.*

HOW DO WE UNDERSTAND OTHERS?

One of the most difficult types of relationships that I've seen is extroverted parents with introverted children. An extrovert is always blurting things out and thinking out loud, whereas an introvert is continuously processing. More often than not, an extroverted parent's definition of being popular and social is pain to an introverted child. Great parents can—and will—step out of their own way and outside their box, look at their children, and say, "Hey, they're happy being by themselves, reading or working on an assignment."

It is certainly possible for extroverts and introverts to get out of their own forms of communication and learn to understand one another. There's an excellent book by Marti Olsen Laney, Psy.D, on this subject that I recommend for families with both extroverts and introverts: *The Introvert Advantage: How to Thrive in an Extrovert World*. It contains great strategies to help introverts successfully live in what is primarily an extroverted world.

Like the extrovert-introvert family relationship, understanding that people are having different experiences than you are is critical to becoming a great leader. A study from the Myers-Briggs Institute estimated that 75% of the population is extroverted and 25% is introverted. Yet, it's also important to be aware, as Linda Silverman, a clinical psychologist from the Gifted Development Center discovered, that 60% of gifted children are actually introverted and that the percentage of introverts appears to increase with IQ. As an extroverted parent, you may like it when your kids are socializing, but kids who are in the library, well, they're obviously doing okay, too!

In order to address this different dynamic in the professional arena as a Vistage International Chair and speaker, I've learned that if I randomly go around the room asking for a response and start with an introvert, I'm not going to get anything—introverts just aren't generally capable of quick, reactive thoughts. Instead, I engage introverts by asking them to give some thought to what I'm asking; then, I'll come back to them later after they've had time to process. An extrovert's error is in thinking everyone should be quick, living every moment in the same, extroverted fashion. Those of us who are extroverts, of course, think we have all the answers!

As I mentioned earlier, I taught a leadership seminar at Walter Payton College Preparatory High School in Chicago. It's a public school that students have to apply to in order to attend based on academic merit. The class took place first thing in the morning, and some of the kids would be at their desks slumped over, heads on their arms. Initially, that body language would have said to me they're tired, sleeping, or uninterested, but the school allowed the kids to be kids. All of a sudden, a hand would go up even though the head would still be down. As it turned out, the kids were right there with me, but were just processing everything and being in the moment in their own way. So, even though you can try to accurately read body language, in that case, I would have read it wrong. It's about understanding how kids learn, instead of forcing them to sit up straight. What are we trying to teach them—how to sit rigidly in a chair? How's that going to serve them? How do you measure success for yourself and your children? If there is a difference, how do you talk about it? How do you define success, and how are you defining significance?

Whether they're right or wrong, we all have opinions and ways of processing and learning. What's important is understanding and being sensitive to the differences. In order to do that, we have to step outside ourselves and really pay attention to those around us. Watch and listen to how people learn: in Little League, in family, and in business. Only then can you effectively be present and truly operate in the moment.

ARE YOU A VICTIM OR AN OWNER?

Victims react, allowing life to happen to them, whereas *owners* have the mental and physical capacity to live their lives all in. If I had only had this awareness in an earlier stage of my life! Owners take responsibility of their life, and victims fall easily into the trap of blaming others.

As my parents tried to deal with their "underachieving child," part of my high school experience included attending a small private preparatory school—the Woodmere Academy (currently, the Lawrence Woodmere Academy) in New York. Here, I became a big fish in a relatively small pond. During this phase of my life, I was labeled an underachiever; today, I probably would have been diagnosed with Attention Deficit Hyperactivity Disorder (ADHD). It was an interesting phase of my life. I went to boarding school for a year, and I hated it. I then ended up at the Woodmere Academy, which was a private day school, so I lived at home.

During my second month at Woodmere, a hurricane hit the East Coast and knocked the power out for 24 hours. Of course I thought, "Cool, the lights are out, so I don't have to do my homework!" Was I ever in for a surprise. The next day, I walked into class, and I was the only one who hadn't done the homework. It wasn't significant to me at the time—realizing I came up with an excuse that led to not doing homework while everybody else in class, whether by candlelight or by flashlight, figured out how they could get their homework done. I had made excuses and became a victim, while the rest of my classmates took responsibility and became owners. Looking to excuses, instead of coming up with creative ways to solve the problem, was a lesson that showed up a lot bigger for me later on.

Life lessons had a way of popping up again and again, one such instance taking place during my high school football years. Coach Bob Weinhauer, who went on to coach a great University of Pennsylvania basketball team that went to the Final Four, was both my football and basketball coach. Two things stand out from that experience. My senior year, I became the starting quarterback. We lost the first two games, and I wasn't playing well because I didn't have much confidence in what I was doing. However, during the third game, there was a change of tides, and I scored the winning touchdown on the final play of the game. We won! I was the hero to all my schoolmates. After the game, while I was walking across the parking lot toward the football locker room, I saw Coach Weinhauer coming toward me. I wasn't sure what he was going to say. As we crossed paths, he just looked at me and said, "You can do better," and walked away. Although his response took me aback, the reality was, I knew he was right.

Over my career, I've thought deeply about Coach Weinhauer's comment. We've talked about goals, the impact of Michelangelo's quote ("The greatest danger for most of us is not that our aim is too high and we miss it, but that our aim is too low and we make it"), and goals being set too high. I've also talked to a lot of people who read the same quote and said, "I'd rather set my goals 'realistically' so I can feel good about achieving them." I've wrestled with this difference. Is there a right or a wrong? I'm not sure there is. I do know that if Coach Weinhauer had told me "Great game, and good job," he probably would have lost his credibility and my respect. Instead, he gave it to me straight. We both knew that I could have played better, and we connected at that level, around honesty and a piece of truth. When I talk later about Patrick Lencioni's "Five Dysfunctions of a Team," it all starts with trust. And trust stems from speaking your truth. Coach Weinhauer didn't try to blow smoke up my butt—he told me his truth.

One of Coach Weinhauer's gifts was being a great orator, the kind of coach that players would run through walls for. Woodmere Academy was a small school, so most of us played offense and defense. It was really striking when, after the last game of our senior year football season, he walked into the locker room and, without saying a word, put up a sign that said, "What I had, I gave. What I kept is lost forever." And that has resonated with me throughout my entire life. What I took away from that was if I missed the tackle and I only gave it 90%, I'd never know how I could have impacted that play. However, if I gave a 100% and didn't make the tackle, I could always feel good about the effort I put forth. Sometimes, that's the best you can do!

I wasn't quite sure of the significance of that then. But as I've looked at successful people and I've looked at the victim-versus-owner mentality, what it really means to me is, "All you can do is the best you can do. Own it." It ties everything together in my life so my goal every year is, *Be 100% in the moment 100% of the time because if I'm not, I'm setting myself up as a victim.* I'm not sure when it connected for me or even if it's the same thing that Coach Weinhauer was saying on the football field, but it is what I practice and how I coach others.

If we're engaged with people and our story is "we're not smart enough," chances are we're not going to be fully engaged. Instead, we will be running protective strategies based on our self-told stories. The way to cut through the noise is to be conscious of the stories we're telling ourselves.

GIVE IT ALL YOU'VE GOT

I've grown to a point in my life where I define failure as not trying. It goes back to Weinhauer's, "What I had, I gave. What I kept is lost forever." You're either playing all-in, being 100% in the moment, or you're not. How can you move anything forward and not fail? The only way you cannot fail is to make decisions based on the past. Many managers just try to improve upon what they've always done because they can say, "Well, that's the way we've always done it." But once you try to go out and do things differently, there's no assurance of success. You're going out into unchartered waters. In order to move anything forward, you have to accept failure.

Most people define failing in such an inhibiting way. If you're only focused on doing the things that you're sure of succeeding at, how many things can you do? Alternatively, I know when I'm teaching my children (or grandchildren) to ride a bicycle, they're going to fail until they learn how to do it. Failing is falling off. If you define it that way, failure turns into not getting back on the bike and trying again.

More often than not, fear of failure stems from the stories we've been telling ourselves since we were children. Like many of you, I fell prey to insecurities and inaccurate self-told stories early in my life. Every week, my family and I did *The New York Times* Sunday crossword puzzle together. The four of us would be in the car; my dad driving, my mom in the front seat, and my brother next to me. My role in this weekly event was the "scribe." Because of my label, I didn't think I could come up with any of the answers. Occasionally, I'd come up with a sports answer. However, most of the answers would be something like Lake Tanganyika in Africa, and somebody else would blurt out the answer, as we successfully completed the puzzle. As a result of the story I was telling myself—that I wasn't very smart—I rarely contributed to coming up with answers and never ventured to take on *The New York Times* crossword puzzle myself. This experience had a trickle-down effect, and I lived my label throughout my school years.

If we're engaged with people and our story is "we're not smart enough," chances are we're not going to be fully engaged. Instead, we will be running protective strategies based on our self-told stories. The way to cut through the noise is to be conscious of the stories we're telling ourselves.

I have the pleasure of working with a lot of amazingly successful people in the business world. Even at this level, I can see how many of them operate in a world of "living in the gap." All of that stress comes from one of two places: "I don't have enough," or "I'm not good enough." What are the stories around that?

We all lead our lives based on the story of that five-year-old inside us; it's not until we take off that mask that we live our true lives. I wasn't able to take off my five-year-old mask until I took an IQ test when I was 23 that informed me I was just as "smart" as my brother. Up until that point, "I wasn't smart; I wasn't good enough," was my story, as I was comparing myself to my brother who has total recall abilities. Armed with this new information, I was able to reframe my story: "I'm not the underachiever." I realized that school wasn't structured for the way I learned. I was a creative thinker, but school was trying to put me in a box. Forcing me to sit down and do rote memorization just wasn't my mode of learning. My mode is learning concepts. Even in college, if I took a course where testing was through multiple-choice exams, I never did well. If it was through the use of concepts, constructs, and ideas, I could readily share ideas and contribute to the discussion.

Now, armed with life experiences and different self-talk, I tackle *The New York Times* crossword puzzle. I sit down and sometimes I can even complete it by myself—my story has changed. What's your five-year-old story?

It's important to recognize that at some point in your life, this story probably served you, but if it doesn't anymore, what do you need to rewrite?

Where are you now in your life? Are you getting what you want? If not, what's your story around that? What changes do you need to make? As Marshall Goldsmith wrote, "What got you here won't get you there!"

IT'S NOT ALL ABOUT MONEY

Recently at a holiday party, one of my Vistage International members I had been coaching for about three years gave a toast. The toast was to me, and he opened up with, "I don't know how you do it, Bob. With all the one-on-ones that you do and as busy as you are, there's never a time I call when you're not available. If you're in a meeting, you get back right to me after the meeting. If not, you're usually back in touch within five or ten minutes." He couldn't believe all that I do.

In response I said, "For one, I don't have children living in my house right now, so I have that availability. But it also feels so good to help people—to get a call and it's someone who wants to bounce an idea off me or get advice regarding a business decision." Whatever the need, it just feels good to help. So I don't want to delude anybody—I'm doing all of this for me!

All quipping aside, there is truth in the benefits of helping others. A lot of people I know read the book *The One Minute Manager* by Kenneth Blanchard and Spencer Johnson. However, I haven't met many people who read the follow-up book by Spencer Johnson: *The One Minute Sales Person*. There is a quote in the book that struck me and has stayed with me ever since: "I have more fun and enjoy more financial success when I stop trying to get what I want and start helping other people get what they want." I've certainly found this to be especially true in my personal and professional life.

As a young Vistage International Chair, I think I had been facilitating a CEO group for about nine months when I had the fortune of having Peter Schutz, who led the turnaround at Porsche, come into my meeting as a resource speaker. To put the scene in context, Peter was probably crusty in his thirties, and here I was catching him in his sixties. Upon walking into the room, he took one look at all of the goals and financial measurements written on whiteboards and asked, "Bobby, what are those?" I responded that they were the goals of my members' companies.

Peter took one look in my direction and said, "They suck." With a smile on my face, I asked him what he meant by that, and without missing a beat, he replied, "There's not one word about the customer." He was right.

In support of Peter's observation, my experience over the last twelve years has been that those companies that focus on making money typically fall short of their goals. Conversely, the companies that focus on adding value to the customer or the community are typically the ones that make or even exceed their financial goals. Take, for example, Southwest Airlines. Southwest clearly identified that success for them wasn't just about making money. Instead, they focused on getting their planes in the air, providing on-time service, and taking care of customers. It wasn't about being the most financially successful company or setting the record of a 20% return on investment. Taking care of what they do best—providing top-notch service along with flawless execution—guaranteed the other.

I have one CEO who takes a great deal of pride in teaching and in giving to others—sometimes to his advantage, and sometimes to his detriment. During downturns, it's very difficult for him to let people go, and he overpays people because he's such a giving person. This puts a real financial burden on the business. Yet in spite of all of this, one summer he took a couple of months off from his own business to help manage another company's stockyard that was in disarray. When I asked him why he did this, he explained it to me this way: "Somebody who's a friend, when you call them for help, is going to ask you, what do you need? Somebody who is a good friend, when you call them for help, is going to show up at your door. Real giving is when you can give without expecting anything back, when you give because the joy is in giving."

However, just as it is important to give, it is also important to know when to receive. Yes, even though I can't "see" you, I know many of you are cringing at the thought of receiving! Perhaps we've all had the old adage "It is better to give than to receive" pounded into us all too often. It can be almost painful to watch people who prefer giving awkwardly take in and receive help or gifts from others. It's interesting because these individuals get such pleasure from giving, yet they generally can't stop and say, "Why wouldn't I want to give the pleasure I experience in giving to others, to somebody else?" What is it about the spotlight that make people try to push it away?

The concept of being selfish, in and of itself, is not a bad thing. All it means is to "do for self." I've seen this a lot. Now, can you get into trouble if you take for yourself at the detriment of somebody else? Of course you can! Can you get in trouble if you only put others before yourself? I believe you can.

One of my favorite metaphors for taking care of yourself was delivered by the late comedian George Carlin; "When you're traveling in an airplane, put the mask on yourself first and then put the mask on a child or somebody who's behaving like a child." It's so good, in fact, that many airline attendants still use it in their preflight briefing to this day.

How many people put themselves at risk rather than take care of themselves, so they can really take care of others? Do you?

LIVING YOUR BELIEFS AND MORALS

Living all-in also requires living within your own beliefs and morals. I've looked back for a long time on a couple of situations that took place while I was the Vice President of Merchandising and a partner at Milgram Kagan. In the early 1980s, Milgram Kagan was the largest independently owned retail shoe chain in the United States. Two moments stand out from this experience.

The first took place while we were in our buying season. That Friday was going to culminate in a weeklong buy where we were going to submit purchase orders in the millions. As the Vice President of Merchandising, I was responsible for signing off on and approving all the buys of the company. Also, my closest friend's wife was having cancer surgery that same Friday. Without hesitation, I made the decision—my place was to be with my friend. I've revisited this decision over time to try to decide whether I handled it correctly or not. I'm still not totally certain. However, I did conclude that if I had to ask the President if I could take the day off, I ran the risk of his saying no. Ultimately, I was unwilling to take that risk.

With my decision made, I prepared the buys and decided to go in on the following Saturday to make sure that everything was checked out. With that, I went and spent the day where I felt I should—with my friend. There wasn't any contact between the company and me, because it wasn't the days of cell phones, and no one knew how to reach me. Consequently, I walked in to a raging boss on Monday morning. After the worst was over, I sat across the desk from the President and responded with the following, "I just need you to know if it happens again, I would do it again." And I got up and walked out. That was the first time I really tested my own conviction about being willing to accept my own death by being fired—that it was more important for me to live my values. The President could have made the decision to fire me for innumerable reasons; however, I chose to do what I felt was the right thing for me. And so, as I coach other people based on this concept, I continue to live all-in, just like Carole challenged me to change in order to enhance our relationship.

The second moment that stands out in my career at Milgram Kagan took place after we sold the company. While it was privately held and we were investing our money, the decisions of expansion were done smartly—very rarely did we make an investment that didn't produce a good return. After the sale, when we were playing with other people's money, some decisions were made to buy companies that we probably shouldn't have bought. In many cases, we were lying to people and telling them we were going to make a good faith acquisition; instead, we would come in and dismantle the company, cut salaries, or make other harsh business decisions.

I swiftly realized the situation just didn't feel good to me. I think Carole might have suggested that at the time I was clinically depressed. I'm not sure whether I was, but I'll buy her diagnosis. In order to break away and clear my head, Carole and I flew to my brother's house in Upstate New York, where we sat on the porch and just talked it through. Breaking my contract was going to cost me six figures, and in the Berk family, if you're going to pay six figures for something, you're going to want to live in it! Ultimately, I made the decision to walk away. I could take in all the advice in the world, but it was my decision. I wasn't sure what I was going to do or how I was going to earn a living, but I was fortunate enough to have Carole's support. She reassured me, "You'll figure this out—we'll figure this out. But you can't stay in a place that makes you miserable."

I've coached a lot of people over the years, with these experiences in mind. It's about living with integrity. It's not worth it to live outside your own beliefs and morals. And if the culture of the organization and the ethics of the corporation don't fit, staying is too expensive of a price to pay.

I would ask you to visit your own situation. If your first instinct is to say that you don't have the luxury of choice—I've already heard it. "It's a tough economic time." "I won't be able to find a job." "I've got kids in school." I get it, but keep in mind, it's a high price to pay.

If you used an assessment tool, such as the OADTM survey, DiSC® profile, EQ assessment, or StrengthsFinder, take a moment to revisit your results. Are your perceived behaviors in line with your actual traits? Do they represent who you are at your core? Are you taking on work in your life that doesn't resonate with you?

How can we play all-in when we're living outside of our ethical and moral values? How can we play all in when we're keeping secrets? How can we play all in when we aren't being authentic? Where do you fit in? Are you living in alignment with your beliefs and morals?

CONTROL IS AN ILLUSION

My first Vistage International group meeting as a chair was scheduled for September 12, 2001. I had my agenda down to finite details and was completely prepared for what I was going to discuss. Then, the events of September 11, 2001 struck.

After 9/11, clearly the right thing to do was to abandon the script and talk about the events of the day before. The work of member groups can be so powerful that one of my members, grounded on a plane in Denver, Colorado, rented a car and drove overnight because he wanted to process the day's events with his group. It was the place where he felt most safe and the place where he wanted to talk through the tragic events of the day.

What followed was an incredibly passionate discussion. We had a Vietnam War veteran within the group who associated the events to his issues around the war. It had triggered feelings surrounding how he was treated when he came home. He shared with the group some of his struggles with the fact that the people inside the World Trade Center were viewed as heroes versus the way he was treated coming back from Vietnam. As member after member contributed, it turned into a powerful 360 discussion of how 9/11 impacted everyone within the group.

For me, the recognition after the events of 9/11 was, no matter what I did, I couldn't keep my kids safe (I'll revisit this later). More broadly, the realization was that control is really just an illusion. And for those of us who think we can control things, there is evidence all the time that we can't, and I think part of people's stress is built around that.

After the meeting was over, I asked the group to give me some feedback, as this was my first meeting. To my surprise, one of the members told me I did a lousy job of time management because we didn't cover the agenda that was laid out. Welcome to the world of chairing and trying to facilitate a group of sixteen CEOs.

Unfortunately, the person who made that statement ultimately died of cancer. That process was also an interesting journey for me, being his coach and Vistage International Group Chair. I was fortunate that somebody suggested I read a book called *Final Gifts*, which was written by two hospice nurses, Maggie Callanan and Patricia Kelley, on how to be around people who are facing death. It was not something I had ever experienced and certainly not something I had ever experienced in a coaching situation. Carole liked to work with the terminally ill because the masks come down, the people are vulnerable, and the real truth comes out. The advice in the book stood out for me in this regard because it talked about how the terminally ill want us to be honest and open. The lesson I took from the book is to be "me."

One of the final times I saw this member, we shared a special moment in his home. He was down to about 80 pounds and had tubes coming out of his body in all directions. Now, I am pretty playful, but I wanted to honor him by being my authentic self, and as I often say, I have no filter. So I walked in, took one look at him, and remarked in a playful manner, "Jesus Christ, you look like shit." And he just burst into laughter.

He eventually responded, "I'm laughing, but it's starting to hurt." His laughter went to tears, and his tears brought me to tears. We shared a real moment, and he thanked me. It goes back to what I was sharing about Coach Weinhauer's remarks. A lot of people were telling him, "Oh, you look good," "You're going to be okay," and so forth. But the reality was, he didn't look good, and he knew he wasn't going to be okay.

What he shared with me during our visit was both interesting and eye-opening. He said to me, "Bobby, I never should have left the first marriage because the same crap showed up in the following three marriages." What he had come to realize, in his fourth marriage, was that the same stuff he left the first marriage for showed up in marriages two, three, and four. What he finally came to realize was he was part of the problems that arose within each one of his relationships. As a result, the same issues kept showing up with whomever he married.

Over my career, what I've suggested to people who come to me and say they're not happy at their work is not to run away from it. Try to fix the problems that exist at work. Then, after you've played all-in at work, if you can't fix it, then it's time to think about leaving. If you leave for certain problems—if you run away—the problems are going to show up again wherever you go next. I think Michelle Saul said it best: "If you run from your demons, they will follow you everywhere. If you run from your demons, when they come back, they bring their big brother."

When I'm working with somebody in a one-on-one situation and they bring up someone else's behavior, it never serves either of us to have that discussion. The only time I've been successful in getting anybody else to change is when I've changed my behavior toward that person. Trying to change someone else, according to Michelle Saul, "is like taking poison and hoping that the other person dies." It's not about control. *It's about the conversation and what changes.* The only thing you can do is control what you want to say. There's a difference between what you can control and what you can change. Having just one conversation isn't going to change things. You have to keep living that conversation 100% of the time.

ALWAYS ADD VALUE TO THE BEST OF YOUR ABILITY...SOMETIMES

Another key thing I've learned while being a chair is that my goal, with sixteen CEOs sitting around the table, is to make sure I contribute value. I still believe that CEOs wake up the day of the meeting with a desk full of business to attend to and that driving to the group meeting, they likely think to themselves, "Why am I doing this?" With this in mind, my hope is that at the end of the day, they leave our meeting thinking, "That was worth it!" What I learned quickly is that trying to give everybody value is not my responsibility. Giving the best I can, showing up, playing all in, and being committed to my part 100% of the time are my responsibilities.

When we perform reviews after a speaker presents, it's interesting to observe how individuals respond. Sometimes individuals will really applaud the speaker, usually if the speaker agrees with their view of life. On the other hand, when speakers challenge beliefs, I have observed how CEOs split into two groups: some go to a place of curiosity and learning, and some go to a place of resistance.

In her book, *Fierce Conversations*, Susan Scott introduces a concept she calls "beach ball reality." This is when an individual experiences the world around them through the colored section of the beach ball they are on. In line with this concept, are we curious when people challenge our different thoughts? Or, does it puff us up when speakers come in and talk about the things we agree with?

Soon after my meeting with Peter Schutz, I was facilitating another group meeting where some of the older members were trying to help a young CEO. They were aggressively pushing him on a few issues when all at once, his body language visibly went into protection mode. He pushed his seat back a little bit from the table, he crossed his arms in a defensive position, and his facial expressions sort of went blank. They were coming at him so hard and heavy that he clearly couldn't take in the information that was being fastball-pitched at him. Diving in, I put my hand up in a "T" and said, "Come on, guys, time-out."

Instantly, one of the tenured members glanced over, pointed his finger at me, and said, "Sit down, shut up, and get out of the way." Now I'm sure there was probably a better way he could have handled that, but he certainly accomplished his outcome, as I took a seat in the corner. I'm not sure, but I might have been sucking my thumb at that point!

After the meeting was over, one of the members came up to me and said, "You did a really good job today."

A bit flabbergasted, I asked, "What meeting were you at?"

And he said, "No, sometimes a finely-tuned sports car just needs a gentle touch on the wheel."

I don't think I've had many "ah-ha" moments in my life," And over the next three or four months, I would check in with members after a meeting and I'd ask, "What did you think of the last meeting?" Invariably, if I thought it was a great meeting, most of them thought it was merely fair. In complete contrast, if I thought it was a fair meeting, they thought it was a great meeting.

What I learned is that I am very comfortable in the spotlight. As I indicated, I've always been the captain of the team or the leader of the organization. As a result, as long as I was working the agenda or was in the front of the room doing the work, I felt great. Consequently, my members weren't getting the value. Conversely, when I was flexible with the schedule and sort of "let it happen" and let them engage, they loved it. And eleven years later, I still leave a lot of meetings with an empty pit in my stomach, but I know it's been a good day. I may not have met my agenda; however, I am confident in the fact that I've provided an opportunity for my members to do good work.

Those of us who like to be in the spotlight can probably grow a lot more by stepping out of it once in a while, and those of you who tend to be in the shadows could probably build your résumé by seeking out the spotlight more often. Ultimately, it gets back to those stories we tell ourselves.

If we look at ourselves, our biggest development and growth is after we've gone through failure or hardship. That's when we change as a person. If you think back on your big growth spurts as an individual, in most cases (if not all), it comes from a negative situation: you get fired, you fail at a job, you don't do well on a test, you break up with a significant other, or you get set back in some other way.

Personally, development doesn't happen unless I feel it in the pit of my stomach. You have to feel it physiologically—you have to know a change has taken place. That's the difference between learning and development. Learning is when you get new information, but development is when you change as a person. That development usually creates personal discomfort. It's that counterintuitive thinking and times when you're confronting and giving up control when it's difficult to be 100% in the moment. For me, it was giving up an act in order to be authentic with my terminally-ill member. Or in another instance (and this is where "sometimes" comes in), it's giving up the power in the room, and "sitting down and shutting up," to allow others to be in control and do the work.

Whenever you see yourself settling into old behavior, stop and check in with yourself. If you are doing this, take a moment to once again revisit your core traits from whatever assessment tool or survey you took. It's important to be aware that your traits sometimes serve you and add value, and sometimes they get in the way. Your biggest strengths ARE your biggest weaknesses; emotional intelligence is understanding the distinction.

BEING A SERVANT LEADER

For me, development is at its best when I'm "adding value" to the lives of my coaching clients, friends, and family at the highest level. Universal law suggests you get paid back in kind through how you conduct yourself and what actions you take. People will often share stories of how they did something nice for someone other than themselves, not expecting anything in return, and yet, a kind gesture or favor was in some way returned to them. You can call it karma, but I prefer to define it as being a *servant leader*.

A fellow Vistage International Chair, Elisa Spain, accuses me of doing too many things for free. The truth is, I take immense pleasure in giving to people. These acts get repaid in many different ways. For example, my family started *A Giving Heart Foundation*, an organization whose mission is that no child should ever have to face open heart surgery, and without hesitation, many people, friends, family, and business connections alike have stepped up and written checks in support.

The biggest lesson that I have learned about being a servant leader is trusting in the power that it brings into your life. When you don't expect other people to repay you, you just give without any hooks. It seems like such a foreign concept to many people because they don't know what to do with it or how to accept what comes back to them. Being a servant leader is about truly being "in service" to people as close to 100% of the time as possible—focusing on helping your friends, family members, or customers and eventually, finding true joy.

A great analogy for being a servant leader is the difference between the Dead Sea and the Sea of Galilee. The Dead Sea in Israel is dead, with nothing growing or alive within its waters. However, the Sea of Galilee on the other side of the Jordan River is prosperous and alive with fish and vegetation. What's the difference? The difference is the Dead Sea only *takes water in* from the Jordan River—nothing goes back out. On the other hand, the Sea of Galilee *takes water in and gives it back out.*

In your life, where are you just "taking in," where are you giving out, and where is there an opportunity to have more richness in your life by giving more?

EMBRACING FORGIVENESS

Another key to bringing more joy into your life lies in the concept of *forgiveness*. If you don't forgive, harboring old angers and resentments, you can't play all-in, because there'll always be a part of you that's not "in." It's as simple as that.

In Jewish tradition, during Yom Kippur, it's common practice to ask for forgiveness from the people you have wronged and to forgive those who have hurt you. In line with this concept, I've tried to live my life with forgiveness toward people and have even worked hard to extend that forgiveness to individuals who do heinous things. I'm talking about what would typically be viewed as evil acts, like hurting children or committing murder. When somebody does something that is so completely unconscionable as this, they have to be sick. Human beings can't consciously do things like that and be well. And when you're dealing with people who are sick, it's much easier to be compassionate, less judgmental, and more forgiving. I have found as I have shifted that in my world, I've had a lot more understanding and, as a result, a lot more joy.

I had a group member who was struggling with his sister's drug addictions. No matter how he tried, he couldn't understand how she could throw her life away through drug use. He was really viewing the situation from a place of judgment. During that meeting, I asked the group to take out a piece of paper and list their addictions. I think we came up with over a hundred—addicted to being right, addicted to consuming sugar, addicted to having the answers, and so forth. Everyone listed every addictive behavior they could think of that gets us into trouble, and that exercise led into an open conversation about them. I think at the end of the day, he wasn't necessarily in a place of forgiving his sister, but there was a small shift in that he was more apt to try to help her. And in order to help her, he really had to let go of his judgment.

It's important to keep in mind that living life in anger and judgment will only serve to make you feel like you're being judged in return. And as soon as you feel you're being judged, your defensive tactics go up, much like the *Starship Enterprise* that I referenced earlier.

Giving in to anger and judgment merely makes you lose your focus and effectiveness, and you just stay angry. How does that serve you? Why spend all of your energy being angry when it is better spent on other resourceful endeavors?

LIVE YOUR LIFE THE WAY YOU WANT TO BE REMEMBERED

If you ask most people how they want to be remembered (what's their significance) or if you look at the writing on tombstones, there is very little about success in business. When two of my highly successful Vistage International members came back as guests after having successfully sold their businesses, both of them shared with the current group members, "If I had to do one thing differently, I would have spent more time with my kids as they were growing up." Both of them had been incredibly passionate about their businesses, and both had held the belief that their personal identities were tied up in their businesses. At one point, one of the members even shared with me that he would never sell his business because that's who he was. However, after they both sold their businesses, they realized that wasn't true, and their biggest regret was that story they had told themselves.

So, what's the story you are telling yourself about how you have to make money or have to be successful in some material way versus making that life-balancing or life-blending choice?

Growing up, many of us heard the statement, "Write your obituary, and live your life as you want to be remembered." It's not a bad exercise. If people live their lives based on what they'd write for their epitaphs, what would they want to be? It's probably that they want to be a good husband, wife, father, mother, or they want to leave an imprint or a legacy. In reading the epitaphs of the captains of industry, you may read how they were the heads of charities and foundations, how they gave back, and the good they have done. Very rarely is it about business.

What is your epitaph? Are you living your life in support of greater life balance, or are you just worried about making money and having material success? That's why I continually coach from a standpoint of designing your life first and then working your business into it. How many people do you know who design their businesses and try to make their lives fit into them? Sure, they may have their successes, but where is their significance?

WHAT DOES LIVING ALL-IN MEAN TO YOU?

Really spend some time on what living all in means to you. What would your life be like if you lived 100% in the moment with the people who are important to you in life or doing what is important to you in business? If you really went at it all-in, how could you change the trajectory of the other things that you want? How would you be able to answer the questions that were posed to you in the introduction? I encourage you to take a moment to revisit these questions:

- Are you on a path to the life you want to live?
- Do you have joy in your life?
- Are you living a life of significance?
- Are you living a life in alignment with who you are?
- Are you living somebody else's life?

It's time to be honest with yourself. Are you truly getting what you want out of life, or is it time to do some work?

CHAPTER FOUR
BE CURIOUS-MINDED

Realizations, both in our personal and professional lives, often don't come to us in the way we expect. To this day, I remember passionately thinking to myself, "Don't take the pills, it's a government conspiracy!" Carole and I were sitting in the movie theater watching *A Beautiful Mind*, the biographical drama based on the life of Dr. John Nash, a Nobel Laureate in Economics. The scene takes place after Dr. Nash is released from the hospital and he is sitting in his den. He opens up his desk drawer and there are about twenty pills in the drawer. It becomes clear that Dr. Nash had not been taking his medication.

As I mentioned previously, I was a political science major and my wife Carole, a licensed clinical psychologist. My mind immediately focused on a government conspiracy, while Carole's instinct was to observe that Dr. Nash was schizophrenic and in need of treatment. As a result of our different worldviews, we sat next to each other in the movie theater, sharing popcorn, watching the same movie, and yet, we had two entirely different experiences.

Later, when Carole and I were sitting, having a glass of wine and debriefing the movie, I asked her, "How did you know Dr. Nash was a schizophrenic?"

She simply responded, "Well Bobby, didn't you see that the little girl in the movie wasn't getting older?"

Surprised, I said, "No, I didn't see that."

The bottom line was, that detail didn't support my story. That was a real 'ah-ha' moment for me—coming to the recognition I was filtering and interpreting the movie through the lens of my professional background and field of study. Alternatively, Carole was filtering the events of the movie based on her professional background and was able to recognize Dr. Nash's schizophrenic behavior.

It takes us back to Susan Scott's beach ball analogy. I was on my own section of the beach ball and was seeing the movie through the worldview of a political science major. Whereas Carole's worldview was another color, and she was seeing the events unfold through the eyes of a clinical psychologist. Everyone looks at the world from the perspective of their own "beach ball reality."

Had I immediately defended my position that it was a political conspiracy, I wouldn't have been open to hear Carole's observation regarding the little girl. Could I see that the little girl wasn't aging? No, because it didn't support my story or the color of my world. But because I approached the conversation from a place of curiosity I was able to acknowledge, "Oh wow, I missed that!" I wasn't caught up in defending my position or trying to sell it as a political conspiracy.

How many of us think and make decisions based on our background, learning, or upbringing, and then try to sell our ideas as being right? Are you aware of the filters that drive your decisions? What's the color of your world? Are you able to see anything else?

As an exercise to heighten awareness of this perspective, I like to give my coaching clients often referred to as an F-test. If you haven't taken this test before, I encourage you to take it. It may open your eyes to how you view things that are right in front of you.

Turn to page 159 to take the F-test now.

Interestingly, even though every single person reading this book will read the exact same paragraph, containing the exact same number of F's, many of you will come to different conclusions as to how many F's are contained within the paragraph. If you look at the paragraph again, you will see that there are, in fact, seven F's. I think the highest correct rate I've seen in any one group is around thirty percent. My guess is that some of those people have been through this exercise before. And it's always fun to watch different personalities come out. In one instance, I couldn't get a chief financial officer from one of my groups to come back into the room for fifteen minutes because he insisted on reading it over and over until he could accurately count all seven F's!

The most important part of this test is not about being right or wrong; it's a matter of what your mind sees. Some of you will not see the F in the word "of" because it sounds like a V, and your mind just skips right over it. Some of you, like me, will see it as a challenge or a game of how fast you can complete the test. And so you might speed through it and not read it closely. People who are really trained well will read it backwards. Again, your story and interpretation of the test will color how you read it and ultimately influence how many F's you count. Everyone is going to see it through their own lens.

I have been told that the Secret Service of the United States is trained to be highly observant whenever they walk into a room. They can observe and remember about 20 percent of what they see. For those of us who haven't been trained that way, the number is typically closer to 10 percent. We catch about 10 percent of what we see and hear before we filter that information through our biases and believe that we have to be right. Then, in our desire to be right, or to show other people how smart we are, we get into trouble in our relationships. Wouldn't we be better off staying curious?

After having experienced this test a couple of times myself, I realize that my F-test with regard to A Beautiful Mind is that I was blind to what was unfolding before my eyes. However, I do give myself credit for having stayed curious, instead of getting into a debate with Carole about the movie clearly being a political conspiracy.

Obviously, at some point in time, somebody in a family or organization has to step up and be the decision maker. The important piece to realize is that the best decisions are based on gathering the insight and perspective of more than just your side of the beach ball.

I was not there, but what I read is that when President Lincoln was preparing to give the Emancipation Proclamation, he called together what would have been his cabinet at that time. He then went around the room to everyone there and he said to them, "Tomorrow I am planning on delivering the Emancipation Proclamation. What are your thoughts?" And everyone in the room suggested that he not do it. To everyone's shock, the next day President Lincoln delivered the Emancipation Proclamation.

After the proclamation was announced, Lincoln's Secretary of State, William H. Seward, stood up and speaking for the group, said, "Mr. Lincoln you've brought us here under great personal hardship and stress. Some of us came by train, some of us came by horse, some of us travelled great distances, and yet you didn't listen to what we had to say." To which Lincoln responded, "I heard everything you said. I just wanted to make sure I had considered everything. Nobody brought up anything that I hadn't thought of. I just came to a different conclusion."

Ultimately, his purpose of bringing his cabinet together was to make sure that he had thought of all the possibilities. His real intent was not to have his mind changed, but to make sure that he didn't miss something. Then, as the president, he owned his decision.

This lesson was one of my biggest development pieces as an effective leader. As the president of the company and the ultimate decision maker, what I ultimately had to learn to do was, before I acted on something, I went to my chief operating officer and asked, "Here's what I'm planning on doing. What might I be missing?"

How do you approach decisions? Are you staying curious? What do others see that you might not? When you do listen to others, how do you listen and respond to feedback from others?

LET GO OF BEING RIGHT (IT'S OVERRATED!)

Where does the need to be right show up in your personal and professional relationships? Have you ever been in a position where you tried to convince someone else that the world is blue, even though they held a strong view that the world is green?

Instead of trying to defend your color, why not be open to hearing what the other person has to say and respect their view? It's time to stop defending your color and let go of being right. Just stay curious, and from that standpoint, see if you can support your position. From there, you'll be better equipped to make informed decisions.

There was an industrial psychologist that came to speak to my Vistage International Chair group who shared a very intriguing message. He claimed to only need one night at the dining room table with a family to see if a family-run business would be successful with more than one generation working in it. He went on to share, if the family operated from a very respectful patriarchal society, where the dad's or mom's word ruled and kids were told to behave because their dad had a tough day at work, then chances were, a family run business wouldn't succeed. However, if the parents remained curious about what the kids were learning and stayed open to the new ideas they were bringing to the table, this was the best indicator that a family business would work. And in today's world, where you have four generations in the workplace at the same time, this balance is more complicated than ever.

As I shared earlier, a senior executive at Edelman is working with a mentor to increase her understanding of the power of social media. Historically, people look to preceding generations for mentoring, however this CEO was able to stay open-minded and turn to a 26-year-old for mentoring. Now that's staying curious!

My son Michael has been my mentor many times over while I was coaching the Flossmoor, Illinois, Bronco League. When I had a tendency to get a little bit out of control on the baseball field, he would always bring me back to reality.

When Michael was ten years old, he went through a brief period where he was getting a little wild with his pitching—which means he was throwing balls instead of strikes. So, in my infinite coaching wisdom, I clapped my hands together and said, "Mike, throw strikes!" He looked at me with a smile and said, "Dad, what do you think I'm trying to do?" Instead of helping Michael find a better balance position or telling him that his arm was dropping down—and giving him *something* that would be helpful—I had tossed out a seriously dumb statement. However, the way that he accepted it and smiled at me helped me understand that my "right" statement wasn't accomplishing anything and there was a better way to step up and coach.

ASKING THE RIGHT QUESTIONS

In his book, *Leadership: Thinking, Being, Doing*, Lee Thayer made the following statement: "If you took away all the tools from a CEO except one, leave him (or her) with the ability to ask the right question at the right time." As Lee so aptly understood, being effective is not about having the right answer; it's about having the *right question*.

I learned this lesson myself as a young executive for Milgram Kagan, a retail business that had stores in northwest Indiana, and northeast Illinois. At a meeting, we decided that we needed to find a way to make money in the first quarter of the year. In January, February, and March of every year nobody was buying regular priced shoes. The only items that were selling at that time of year were sale-priced winter boots. So the company made the decision to do whatever they could to be profitable in the first quarter of the following year. As it followed, we were successful, and it also turned out to be one of the worst mistakes we made! By cutting costs so drastically in the first quarter, it took us longer than expected to recover in the second quarter. Unwittingly, putting those two things together had an unexpected negative impact. We answered the question we asked, but unfortunately, it was the wrong question.

So as we progressed, the conversation switched from how to make money in the first quarter. This led to the question, "Where do you sell regular priced shoes in the first quarter?" which in turn led to our wildly successful "sun and sand belt strategy." The geographic strategy placed fifty percent of our distributions in the sun and sand belt within the next five years, helping to position the company to get an extraordinary value when the company was sold.

Another great example of staying open to asking the right questions arose with one of my Vistage International members. He was the owner and CEO of Pets International Ltd., a company that was continuously winning new product development awards and enjoyed a huge market share in some of the categories it was in. For example, at one point in time he owned close to 40 percent of the domestic market in hamster cages.

The hard truth is, if you don't initiate proactive change, then someone else is going to make a change for you, putting you on the defensive.

I walked into his office one day and asked, "What do you have to do to get to market fifty percent faster?"

He responded, "You don't understand. We get to market faster than all of our competition by a large margin."

I said, "I get that. I see your awards. What would it take to get to market faster?"

We had this debate for about twenty minutes. It got to the point where I even thought he was going to come across the table and harm me.

But he finally said, "I got it." And on Monday morning, he sat down with his product development team and asked them, "What would it take for us to get to market fifty percent faster?"

Interestingly, his team split in their viewpoint when asked the question. Half said it couldn't be done. The other half said, in order to accomplish that level of a change, they would have to look into different manufacturers and think of a new logistics approach. There would also probably be some product failure that would have to be built into their margin structure.

As a result of asking this question, he now knew right away which team members could, and would, help him move the company forward. They never made it to market fifty percent faster, but they did get to market twenty-eight percent faster.

So, how can you challenge and influence a "this is the way we've always done it" mentality? You do it by asking powerful questions. The hard truth is, if you don't initiate proactive change, then someone else is going to make a change for you, putting you on the defensive.

I recently heard a story about a top restaurant in New York City called Le Bernardin. The two chefs, Mauy LeCoz and Eric Riport, at the top of their game, told their investors that they were going to change the way they go to market with the *Prie Fix* menu. The investors were taken aback that, at the top of the market, they wanted to make such a drastic change. In response, the chefs explained that they knew that one day they would have to change and they were currently in the best position to try a new menu because their customers would follow them now. They would be taking a much greater risk when they started to lose market share and popularity.

Tiger Woods is another great example of changing while at the top of your game. During the late 1990s and early 2000s, Tiger was the number one rated golfer in the world, but he felt that he needed to change his swing or the rest of the pros were going to catch up to him. And the next year, he had a terrible year because he was making changes to his game. Then, a short time later, Tiger came back full-force, winning all four major golf tournaments over a 12-month period. That willingness to ask himself how he could improve his game and take a risk enabled Tiger to reach an even higher level of performance.

In today's changing market, everyone talks about change, and it's never change for the sake of change. The real question is, when you look at the way you're doing business or how you are in your relationships, are they getting you the result you want, and will they continue to? Is what you're doing going to get you where you want to go? If not, I propose you consider asking yourself some powerful questions so that you can get going in the right direction.

Here are some basic questions to help you get reflective on staying curious:

- What's working in your life and what's not?
- What part of this are you willing to own?
- What's your accountability and responsibility in this situation?
- If you're not getting what you want, what's your story around that?
- When did somebody do something to you that you're still holding on to?

People have a tendency to blame others. "My mother did this! My father did that!" And that's true, those people probably did. But real growth comes from accepting your responsibility in the situation and taking action. If you can step out of your five-year-old mindset into your mature, grown-up mindset, you won't remain a victim.

As Mark Twain so aptly stated, "If you keep doing what you're doing, you're going to keep getting what you got."

INTRODUCING NEW, DIVERGENT, CREATIVE TYPES OF THINKING

In his book, *Reflections on the Human Condition*, Eric Hoffer eloquently penned, "In a time of drastic change it is the learners who inherit the future. The learned usually find themselves equipped to live in a world that no longer exists." This quote has resonated with me because, I have always believed if you are not green and growing, you are brown and dying.

In the shoe business, it used to strike me that every year, buyers made a perfect buy for the previous year. What I mean by this is, in 1990, if red was the hot color, we would end up short on inventory and it would be costly, under bought. Then, invariably, the buyers would buy a lot of red shoes for the following year, and we'd end up not selling what they over bought. How many times have you found yourself "buying last season's red shoe" instead of trying to determine what the next "red shoe" is? It's human nature to tend to look backward.

An economist once shared with me that human beings have a three-year memory of recovery. We make our decisions looking backwards instead of looking forward. In 2007, we were coming off record growth in home values and stock market growth, so the idea of buying either based on passed trends would have been seductive. However, bad times were coming and the investments would not have panned out. The same can be said after the horrible downturn in 2008. Real estate and stocks plummeted and that would have been a great time to buy. This is about looking forward and using counterintuitive thinking. Many entrepreneurs sell their businesses when values are down and they are not having fun. How much more would they have received for their businesses if they sold when the wind was behind their back and values were high?

Real success and growth come from staying curious and introducing new, divergent, creative types of thinking. A poster child for this way of thinking is the company GAP. In the early 1970s, GAP revolutionized the way the apparel industry came to market. Up to that time, it took roughly 90-120 days for a company to go from design to getting product on the store racks. A new president, Millard Drexler, came to GAP in 1983 and boldly steered the company towards getting new designs on the racks in a record 39 days. He also brought in people who didn't subscribe to the old paradigm and who didn't say it couldn't be done. Some of you may even remember; every Monday, if you went into GAP, there would be new colors and new designs in the store. This model revolutionized the way people did retail. More often than not, it's the one who comes in with divergent, creative ways of thinking that changes a paradigm who wins.

The same divergent thinking is applicable within your family. What are the jobs that are going to be available for your children? They're most likely not going to be the jobs that are available now. Depending on how old your children are, they will be the jobs that will be relevant fifteen or more years from now. It all comes down to preparing your children, and youth in general, for the world that they're *going to live in*, not the one we currently live in.

How often do you find yourself stuck in an old paradigm or stagnant way of thinking?

I had an eye-opening experience with one of my Vistage International members who was marrying a woman whose father was deaf. One day I asked him, "Are you going to learn sign language?"

Puzzled, he responded, "Why would I do that?"

I said, "Out of respect, so you can communicate with your new father-in-law."

To that, he tactfully answered me back, "Bobby, I don't need to learn sign language. We just sit across the table and text each other."

My antiquated way of thinking, that sign language was the only way to communicate fully with someone who was deaf, made me look silly. When in reality, new divergent and creative technology has already shifted how we can communicate. Now, it was a matter of being open-minded and curious enough to embrace the change.

I recently read an article in the *Journal of the Royal Society of Medicine* that discussed genius and how divergent thinking plays a part. Divergent thinking includes the ability to interpret a question in many different ways and the ability to see many different answers to a question. In a study of kindergarteners, 98 percent of them were at a genius level of divergent thinking. Five years later, that genius had already dropped to 50 percent, and five years past that, the number had dropped even further. So, how can we accept and nurture that divergent type of thinking and openly welcome these changes into our families and businesses?

In his book, *Hoop Dreams*, Phil Jackson touches on this subject. As a son of missionaries, Phil was brought up on an Indian reservation. In the American Indian culture, the person who was "different" was viewed with regard and respect because they were change agents. So it's not surprising that when Phil Jackson brought Dennis Rodman onto the Chicago Bulls basketball team, he viewed his unique personality with respect and honor, rather than seeing it as disruptive. Phil was able to integrate Rodman with the other personalities on the team, because he was able to embrace what Dennis Rodman brought to the team.

As a leader at work or at home, that ability to think outside of the box is really what you want to embrace. It's not about accepting what is, but looking at ways to be a change agent in a constructive and positive way. As Henry Ford said, "If I had listened to my advisors, I would have created a faster horse!"

Divergent thinking is also important in families. As parents, we often think we know best; however, when Jenny was pregnant with our first grandchild, she asked us to take Expectant Grandparent Classes at Northwestern Memorial Hospital. I was curious as to why my daughter wanted to take classes since we had successfully raised her and Michael, but after going through the course, I learned new information and became a better grandparent for it. Parents tend to raise their children based on the way that they were raised, but the role of parents is to provide the best care. When we brought our children up we used bumpers and slept our kids on their stomachs; now, the world has come out with new science supporting a different way of thinking by not using bumpers and sleeping children on their backs.

WHERE DO YOU FIT IN? WHERE ARE YOU IN YOUR THINKING?

One important aspect of staying curious is understanding where you fit in and how you are hardwired to think. Having this awareness will allow you to open yourself up to new, divergent ways of thinking where you might otherwise lack.

Revisiting the assessment tools from earlier, it's important to remember that your biggest strength can also be your biggest weakness. The key is to know when it is being used as strength and when it is getting in your way.

For instance, my lead characteristics are being outcome-driven and being liked and right, and my weakest characteristic is patience. So, I know I have to train myself to be more patient. However, there are other traits that I viewed as of lesser importance that I now realize I have to work on equally as much.

When I had the Vistage International chairs interview my kids and Carole, with the goal of being a better husband and better parent, the feedback I received was eye-opening. Carole's feedback was that "Bobby rushes even to relax." Jenny's viewpoint was, "Why do we always have to be the first one on the airplane?" And Michael's input was, "Why does Dad always have to get up and be the first one up from the table?" Although I personally thought they were little things, a strong theme of traits was showing up and apparently impacting my relationships with the most important people in my life.

The playful side of that story is, while I was in the San Diego airport recently, waiting to board my American Airlines flight, I was in line for Starbucks when they called my boarding group. True to my nature, I started to get out of line. But instead, I chose to wait in line to get my coffee, and as a result, I ended up boarding the plane with Group Three. Now I'll be honest, I was slightly panicked, but when I eventually boarded, my seat was still there, and I was able to put my carry-on luggage above my seat. When I called Jenny and told her I had done that, did she ever feel validated.

In another instance, at Thanksgiving dinner a couple of years ago, we had finished dinner and the family was relaxing at the table when Michael asked me, "Aren't you going to get up?" And I said, "I'll die first!" So, just being aware of your traits, for better or worse, and being willing to adapt where needed is half the battle.

What are your traits that you need to keep an eye on? Where could you use some adaptation? Most importantly, are you willing to move into the world of those around you or do you expect them to move into yours? Maybe it's time to ask the important people in your life….

BEING COMFORTABLE IN YOUR DISCOMFORT

Dr. Rick Eigenbrod, a clinical psychologist, explains that development usually comes from our struggles and the places that were hardest for us. As you look back on your career, you will likely notice most of your significant develop did not come from a positive experience.

It's amazing to me how many people equate accomplishment with "doing," where sometimes the higher you go up in an organization the more it's planning and thinking. We often see this in the field of sports. At the end of a player's career, they will often turn to coaching. In this position, they have to redefine what success means to them. Success as a ball player was "getting the hit" at the right time in the game and training properly, whereas success in coaching is about preparing others. And when somebody else is in that glory position, a lot of us feel that we're not contributing because we're contributing in a different way.

That's one of the things that can hold you back in the past and doesn't speak to your own development. Are you willing to go into that unknown, where you don't feel competent because it's a place you've never been before?

I can't tell you how many people are resistant to joining my CEO groups because they don't necessarily see themselves as a CEO. They don't want to join because they don't feel like they fit. Their story is, "Although I'm at the head of the food chain at the organization, I don't really belong here" or "I'm 63 years old and I'm still waiting for adult wisdom."

When Vistage International chairs first come to the position and they introduce themselves as, "I'm a new chair" I always ask, "When do you stop being a 'new chair', and when do you become a 'chair'?" I believe, putting that label on themselves, gives them an excuse for maintaining a certain level of performance. So, anytime someone starts a sentence with a disclaimer, it's usually about his or her own discomfort.

This same concept of discomfort extends into our personal lives as well. The one thing we're supposed to be really prepared for is parenting. Unfortunately, there are no classes on that.

When Carole and I first gave birth to Jenny, the nurse handed her to us after she had her first bowel movement and said, "Do you guys want to clean this?" And we looked at each other and said, "Well, we're going to have to start some time, we might as well start now." Nobody told us a baby's first bowel movement is like black tar! It was all over us and all over her. Talk about discomfort. Our growth and wisdom as parents was, when Michael was born and the nurse asked us, "Do you want to do this yourselves?" We both chimed in, "No, thanks, you can do it."

There are many times in life where you may feel like you are thrown into your position. If you've never been the president before, how do you prepare for this new position? Whether it's Obama or Romney, or another presidential election, take your pick. The first day they're president, they can only imagine what it's going to be like. But once they're in the seat, it's theirs.

It's the same case in any organization or position. When we become husbands, parents, Little League coaches, CEOs, CFOs, managers, or students for the first time, what's the story you're telling yourself about that?

As a CEO, how do you make open-minded and informed decisions, staying comfortable in the discomfort that you might make a mistake? As a Little League coach, how do keep from making it personal, staying focused on the team? As a parent, how do you let your kids fall off their bikes so they can learn?

It's important to realize every decision you make can't be right and you can't protect everyone from their own "learning hurts." True success is about being a servant leader and not making any position about you. It's about staying curious, letting go, and being comfortable in your own discomfort.

If you stop being curious, and you find yourself going into defense mode, just be careful. Instead, I suggest that you stay curious and explore why you feel the need to defend. The fact that you need to defend suggests that you feel somebody is attacking.

Two women in my life that I love and respect, my wife Carole and my friend and mentor, Michelle Saul, have both reinforced with me, "Would you rather be right or be in a relationship?" What is this need to be right all about? Does that mean your loved ones need to be wrong?

Many of our politicians struggle to embrace, or even hear, the viewpoints of their colleagues from the the other party. What does that get them, or us? If you compromise, are you weak? Is this getting you what you want? Are you staying curious-minded in order to make the best decisions?

CHAPTER FIVE
LEAVE IMPRINTS

It's time to get honest with yourself…whose job are you doing? Are you doing your job or someone else's? Just exactly how are you spending your time?

I ask this because, in order to be a great leader, it's critically important to always remain aware of and clear about how you spend your time. One of my members, Glenn Horton, has always said, "The single biggest mistake a CEO can make is if they are not charging forward and they are turning around to pick up the people that are falling behind them."

You can't turn around and slow your growth rate down to go back and pick up people! As shocking as it might sound, you have to keep moving forward, and if the people behind you can't keep up with you, then you have the wrong people.

Earlier in the book, I shared the three-part entrepreneurial triangle, which is at the core of the three levels of leadership. If you recall, at the beginning stage, the bottom of the triangle, everybody's doing everything, and everybody is generally enjoying what they are doing. Then, all of a sudden the CEO will make a move to reach a higher level, moving to the top of the triangle and creating a void, and nature hates a void.

In a perfect world, the people who were working alongside the CEO at the bottom of the triangle would move up and fill that void. But historically and statistically, they don't. If the CEO goes back in to fill a void, doing someone else's job, forward momentum will be brought to a screeching halt.

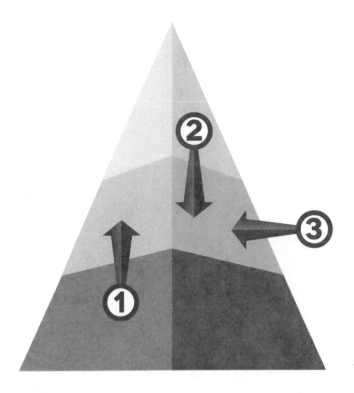

This outside influence can, and will be, stressful for the culture.

If promoting people has a low probability of success and the CEO stepping back in to fill the void doesn't work, the only thing that is left is to bring in talent from the outside—someone who has successfully done for someone else, what you want them to do for you. This outside influence can, and will, be stressful for the culture. Chances are that someone within the current ranks will try and sabotage the new hire. However, the CEO will need to let the friction work itself out, keeping an eye focused on the results.

This whole process begs the question, what's to be done?

Previously, I touched on the concept of "empowerment" that was introduced in Japan and how it saw varied levels of success in the United States. Implementation was most successful where executives empowered other people to make decisions and those people over-communicated up. However, if executives had to go in search of information, they would assume the worst and develop negative thoughts around the situation.

To counter this common tendency, I've always said to people, "Never have a conversation with someone else when they're not present." You'll find, having "absent conversations" typically only leads to filling in the wrong blanks. This also holds true in regards to your kids and family.

An example of this in my life is when I was feeling underappreciated by my son, Michael. When I finally decided I had to tell him how I felt, he responded, Dad, sometimes I feel the same way." I had no idea! Bringing this absent conversation to light, allowed our relationship to grow and be more fulfilled than it ever had been. It created a platform that allowed our relationship to grow then and to continue to grow.

A similar situation arose in business with one of my coaching clients where the Vice President of Operations within the company was flawlessly handling an issue that clearly belonged on his desk. However, simultaneous to the Vice President resolving the issue, the President of the company was walking with the Chairman of the Board, when the Chairman asked about the issue. Unfortunately, the President, not apprised of the situation, was caught unaware and placed in an awkward position with the Chairman. Had the Vice President merely "over-communicated," even if only an "FYI," the President could have been able to communicate to the Chairman that he was aware of the situation and he had every confidence his Vice President had it under control.

A great metaphor for enabling a company to empower individuals and move from the entrepreneurial stage to a more professionally-managed organization is Susan Scott's Decision Tree from her book, *Fierce Conversations*. The first key is to hire the right people. After that, it's about providing clear objectives and getting out of their way.

On the Decision Tree, if the challenge is a "leaf issue," anyone in the organization should be able to make the decision, because leaf issues aren't paramount to the health of the tree and the leaf will grow back. If it's a branch issue, everyone in the organization should still feel empowered to make the decision; however, they should check one level up before executing the decision. Branches can impact many leaves, but the tree itself will still be healthy. If the challenge is a trunk issue, the decision belongs at the executive level, as the trunk impacts all the branches and leaves. In regards to root issues, which can determine whether an organization lives or dies, those belong with the CEO. Alternatively, I've seen CEOs get involved because the carpet in the office is dirty. Is that really where they should be spending their time, on a leaf issue? The key is that anyone should be empowered to get the carpet cleaned.

I remember walking into a meeting at my company and asking a question. One of the attendees responded to me, "Bob, don't you think this is a branch issue?" I thanked the person and walked out. That person was spot on. As I've said before, the best run companies are those where everyone is working at or above their position, not below.

In order to foster empowerment around any interaction, two things need to be clear: the desired outcome and who owns the decision. I can't tell you how many times I've heard, "It's our decision." I would suggest that there is an appropriate time and a place for collaboration and times to seek others' input. Yet, at the end of the day, someone has to own the decision and be account- able for the results. And yes, the decision can be to empower someone else to make the decision. However, in that case, it's important to remember that you still own the outcome.

"Whose job you are doing today?" really comes down to good commu- nication, mastering the language of empowerment, and being clear on who owns the decision.

What types of decisions are you making in your organization or in your family? Conversely, what decisions are you empowering others to make? Are they appropriate?

HOW BETTER LEADERS SPEND THEIR TIME

After the start-up phase comes to a close, it's time for the leader to establish what's expected by setting a clear vision and mission and getting clear on and establishing everyone's roles.

Larry King—not CNN's Larry King—but an outstanding business coach, has established that an effective CEO should spend 80 % of their time in the follow- ing six roles: as Ambassador, Inventor, Investor, Strategist, Student, and Coach.

THE AMBASSADOR

It's widely thought that being an ambassador is primarily about creating rapport and building relationships. Well, I think that's probably true. If you look at how brand ambassadors spend their time, their focus is on building and nurturing relationships with the most important clients and referral bases. It's about sharing your vision and taking it out into the marketplace through public relations, speaking engagements, and visits with your key clients.

Jeff Mariola, former CEO of Ambius in the United States and Europe, shared with me that his goal everyday was to make it easier for their custom- ers, suppliers, and employees to engage in business with his company. And at the end of every day he would ask himself, "What did I do today to be a better ambassador to each of those constituents?"

Do you spend an effective amount of time with your key customers, suppliers, and employees? How about with your family and friends? Are you making it a priority to nurture your most important relationships?

THE INVENTOR

I often see companies that stay with products and systems that are no longer working for them. They work on *improving* operations when the most effective action would be to *create new* operating systems.

So, how important is it for you to update your products and your processes? …very important.

Think about what I shared about Walgreens earlier—how they had the foresight to abandon their food-counters while it was the profit driver of the company. As the President of Walgreens knew, "The job of the CEO is to make your business obsolete before your competition does." In contrast, when did Blackberry fall asleep and lose most of their market share? I learned this when my grandson Mason, three at the time, grabbed my Blackberry and tried to use my phone by swiping his finger across the screen. Samsung and Apple had advanced the technology so much that the next generation wouldn't view cell phones as working without a touchscreen.

I recently met with a family-run company where their revenue has been fairly flat. We started analyzing what was happening by looking at their cost structure. Looking at their Information Technology (IT) resources, I was surprised to see that they had two individuals on payroll to support a staff of thirty. So as I delved into reviewing his IT needs, I asked them if they had ever given any thought to outsourcing their IT versus having two on the payroll. Much like Blackberry, I think they just fell asleep on it. So, I then introduced them to someone who could help them look into outsourcing and to do a risk-reward analysis.

In the same sense, if you're a commodity but you keep producing the same things over and over again, eventually the market's going to drive your price down. If you're in manufacturing, how long before you need to invest in robotics? If you're in the recycling business, what are the new products that are going to be recycled over time? It's about having a constant curiosity about what's next and then timing it right.

What are the new efficiencies, initiatives, markets, products, and new way of doing things that you can embark upon?

Don't overlook your family system either. Be honest with yourself…is it working? Do you always do the same things? Do you always go to Florida on vacation? Are you willing to experiment and try new things? Or, do you get into the habit of redoing things?

What's your role as a leader in that? If, as the leader or head of the family, you like to play golf in Florida, but your children want to go on a skiing adventure, how do you make those choices?

THE INVESTOR

I hear so many times in family-owned businesses that the goal is to sustain the business for future generations. Yet often, the family "guts" the cash out of the business to support a certain lifestyle and then when there is an economic downturn or product failure, they are not in the position to weather the storm. The "investor" must realize that the best way to achieve the stated goal is to make smart decisions as to what to do with the cash flow of the business. If there is positive cash flow, are you paying down debt, reinvesting, and paying dividends in proper proportions?

I've even seen companies give too much to charity based on the financial health of the business. If you're in this position, it's important to realize, you can always give more to charity later when you have improved your balance sheet. This same kind of discipline needs to be applied to family spending.

Belaji Krisnamurthy, Founder and President of LogiStyle, worked for General Electric and other technology companies before launching LogiStyle. And I loved his philosophy. He thought that the first responsibility of a company's CEO is to return value to the investors. Then, once the investors have been paid, the rest of it is like a buffet line. The first person on the buffet line should be the lowest level on the organizational chart. When they have all eaten (they have all made their goals), then, and only then, will their supervisor get to the buffet line (their bonus) and so on up the organization. The CEO is the last one at the buffet table, and if everyone in the company has eaten (earned their whole bonus) then the CEO gets to eat as much as they want.

This is one of the fundamental problems that we're hearing in the marketplace today. If you're taking care of yourself as the CEO, but you're not taking care of your people, what's that about? Wouldn't it be interesting if the only way you could get your bonus is if all your people make their bonuses? Might you approach your job a little bit differently?

The question also begs asking, how are you showing up within your family? Are you taking care of them or yourself?

At one time, I did some recruiting at Northern Illinois University, and it was very clear to me that there were two groups of young adults that we were interviewing. One group knew that if they didn't leave college with a job, they had no place to go for income. Needless to say, they were motivated. On the opposite end of the spectrum were the young adults who knew they had a financial safety net. So, how do you think the majority of the ones in this group valued their education?

During one of my Vistage International group meetings, I conducted a round table with sixteen CEOs, asking each of them, "What is your obligation, if any, to your children in college?" Needless to say, we came up with sixteen different answers. Some people would pay for their children's college education if they could, while others would pay for their children's education only if they got A's or B's. So, each one was different. And so there's no right or wrong. It's just, how do you look at that as a family unit? At what age do the kids get to play a role in that?

THE STRATEGIST

Being an effective strategist requires having vision. Take for instance when NASA said they would land a man on the moon. They weren't shooting for landing where the moon currently was, they were calculating on where it would be by the time the space craft arrived there. The same can be said with regard to *The Wall Street Journal* article I mentioned earlier: the best leaders have the ability to *see around the corner*.

I worked with a hand tool company whose vision was to have a "tool on everyone's home site in the world." Once they focused on their vision, it became clear that an application strategy gave them the best chance at reaching their goals. It also helped establish the company's charitable mission as they started to support Habitat for Humanity.

I believe that every time "strategy and tactics" are discussed, we are really talking about tactics. Strategy is intuitive.

So, how do you move your business forward, whether it's through Jim Collins' *Good to Great* model or another? You can start by attempting to anticipate the changes that are on the horizon.

How do you plan the right strategy? I think the role of a leader is to determine the "why" and "what," and then it's up to the team to determine the "how." People need a clear strategy so they can measure what they're doing. Is your current behavior and strategy getting you where you want to go?

A current example of this arose recently with one of my members. My

> # I believe that every time "strategy and tactics" are discussed, we are really talking about tactics. Strategy is intuitive.

member is the owner of a small, very hands-on, and very strong, operational business. The only assets the family has outside of the business itself are the warehouse where they house their business and a piece of property in Florida. As a result of the real estate downturn, both of those assets are very highly leveraged. One day, she shared with me that she wanted to be able to retire by the time she's 60 years old; however, on the current trajectory, she's going to fall short of that mark. In her case, she's decided to push her retirement goal back to 64 versus taking a risk in order to achieve retirement by age 60. Now, it's not the choice that I'd go with, but its okay to not want to take the risk. You just have to be prepared to alter your goal.

THE STUDENT

As Dr. Rick Eigenbrod said, "No organization can grow faster than its leadership." Think about it. When you were young and starting out in your business there were probably many mentors available to you. However, when you reach the C-suite, the learning curve traditionally decelerates. To counter this, what do you and your leadership team need to do in order to accelerate the learning curve? How can you ramp up your learning so the organization can grow?

Continued growth and learning requires staying open-minded to new ideas, thoughts, and new ways of doing things. For example, if I try to call my son, I may get a call back in a week. However, if I send him a text his response is almost immediate. New ways of doing things can be more effective and receptive to your audience.

I've also had fun conversations with people who are upset we are teaching less handwriting and spelling in school. My playful response to this way of thinking is, "Just think. What if the Egyptians held a similar mindset? We might still be using hieroglyphics as our way of communicating!"

This is where being a student comes in. Being a student means continuously building your skills and staying open to the "new." You shouldn't consider yourself "done" at any level. Life's about continuous growth. As I've mentioned before, you're either green and growing or brown and dying.

THE COACH

As we talked about earlier, your role as a leader is developing your people and making sure they're continuing to grow at a higher level. As Ben Peck, President of Wohl Shoe Company, said, "Build your people and let them build your company." If they can't, even after some coaching, then you need to bring different people into your organization. If people aren't performing, and you allow that in your organization, then you're lacking accountability.

Mike Scott, a leading authority on accountability in the workplace, defines accountability as two things. First, it's about doing what you said you would do, when you said you would do it. Secondly, don't let anybody come to you with problems they don't have at least two solutions for; otherwise, they start training you to solve their problems, instead of taking responsibility. And if you're solving their problems, you're doing their job. A CEO, who I coached for ten years, kept a sign on his desk as a constant reminder to do his job that read, "Whose job am I doing today?"

Revisiting Larry King's six ways a CEO should spend 80 % their time, what would you have to do in your organization so you could focus on being an Ambassador, Inventor, Investor, Strategist, Student, and Coach? How does that compare to your current work week? Do you have people who you can trust to do their work? Have you built a business and a family culture based on trust and accountability?

YOUR ROLE AS A LEADER

Glenn Horton, who made the successful move from entrepreneur to professionally-managed business, after he bought the company from his father, defines the role of the CEO as three things: make sure your business model works, be in on the really big deals, and hire and train the best talent.

The first role of a CEO is to *make sure your business model works*. Is your operational model the most efficient, or should you be looking at that as an opportunity?

I referenced the CEO of a construction company that had to decide whether remaining a union shop or becoming both a union shop and an open shop was a business model question. In another example, when Jack Welch was at the helm of General Electric, he changed their business model from product to service based. During an interview, he was asked how long that would take, to which he promptly came back with, "fifteen years." Metaphorically, as I mentioned before, Jack Welch referenced OODA loop when he said, "if the rate of change outside your business is faster than the rate of change inside your business, you lose."

The rate of change continues to speed up for all of us. Every day, companies are shifting from sales people creating leads to newer more efficient models. With the speed of innovation escalating, you need to stay on your toes and review your business model frequently, as it pertains to your industry sector.

The second role of the CEO is to *be in on the really big deals*. What is the level of sales that you should be involved in? What do you need to bring other interested parties in? Going back to Susan Scott's Decision Tree, what are the leaves, branches, trunk, and roots, in your sales challenges?

If you think about it, in a large law firm, senior partners can typically charge $800 per hour, whereas the junior partners may charge $500, and the first-year lawyer, fresh out of law school, is charging $175. There are some cases that I might want the $800 lawyer working on. There are some cases where the $500 is really good enough. There are also some situations where working with the $175, first-year lawyer, is right where I should be. I would hope if I call the $800 an hour partner, he would say to me, "Bobby you don't need me on this. I'm going to give it to John and I'll be overseeing it." Yet, time and again, I see in general business that most people aren't comfortable allowing a more junior person to take on the job with supervision.

I'm currently coaching a man who is in the sales profession whose earnings are well into the six figures. He was considering becoming the international sales manager, which would require him to travel more frequently. During my interview with him, he mentioned he had a set of ten-year old twins; one of which had a math tutor and the other had a swimming coach. I asked him, "Why don't you tell your kids that you now have a coach? We can give them the opportunity to share what they think you would need to do to become a better dad." He agreed. One of them responded, "You know, I'd like my dad to come to more of my swimming practices. I'd like for dad to be home at the dinner table. I'd also like my dad to tuck me in three nights a week." The other twin came back with, "I'd like to take a vacation with just me and my dad. I'd like to take family vacations. And I'd like him to raise my allowance from $3.50 to $4.00 a week." After reading his children's input, I asked, "Now, tell me why you're going to take this job?" He was speechless…and he took the job.

In contrast, my wife Carole has figured this out. She has purposely shrunk her private practice so she can spend more time with our grandchildren, Mason, Logan, Brayden, Lucas, and Alexis. We are privileged to live close to our kids and are actively involved in their lives. We get to see Mason play soccer and Little League and watch Brayden dance, sing, and romp around the house. We get to watch Logan at her ballet recitals and soon at her T-ball games. We get to take them all swimming…and seeing Lucas and Alexis smiling at me. It's just magical!

Carole (a.k.a. Nana) visits with them on a regular basis, works on projects with them, reads to them, and helps them prepare for the school days ahead. Our grandchildren all know the days of the week. For Mason and Logan it's Sunday, Monday, Nana-day, Wednesday, and so on. For Brayden and Lucas, Wednesday becomes Nana-day. If you ask any of them what their favorite day of the week is they will all tell you, it's Nana-day. We know the time will come when friends and other activities will (appropriately) intrude on this special time and our roles will change, just as they do in business.

Only you can determine what the really big deals are for you and your company and nurture the discipline to stay out of the others. As with many of the concepts in this book, this spans into your family and personal life as well. What decisions are you letting your children make, so they learn about the rewards and consequences around their decisions?

The last role of the CEO is to *hire the best talent*. One of the best examples of this that I have experienced took place within one of my Vistage International groups. The group member in question operated a family business and every time we went through the process of interviewing his direct reports, he always expressed that they were A-Players. However, it was the group's feeling that, at best, these individuals were really B-Players, or even C-Players. To add to this impression, the company never reached any of its goals. The entire group felt he was trying to win the game with the wrong team.

When this person chose to finally leave his family business, I asked him, if he could ethically, morally, or legally take any of his direct reports with him, who would he take? And do you know what he said? Nobody!

After this conversation, I went back to the group with an exercise. I asked the group the following: "If you were in the process of starting a new business, and you could take anyone from your current leadership team with you, who would you take? Interestingly, not a single person answered the question, "Everyone on my team." What was driving that behavior? As I stated before, it's my belief that A-people hire A-people and B-people hire C-people. A-people are comfortable with associates or direct reports as smart as or smarter than themselves. However, B-people don't want that level of challenge.

If asked this same question, what would you do? If you wouldn't take your entire leadership team with you, why are you tolerating them today?

Working with your team and being a good Coach, hiring the best talent, or getting in on the really big deals isn't going to come to fruition unless you have the right people executing. And if you don't have the right people executing, then doesn't it make sense that you, as the CEO, are going to have to go back in and *do somebody else's job*, and doesn't that *stop the organization from moving forward*? Now granted, sometimes you may need to go back in and do someone else's job, just be careful to make it short-term and make sure you have an exit plan when you go in.

WHERE DO YOU SPEND YOUR TIME?

If you believe in Larry King's fundamental approach, how much of your current time is being spent in these six ways: Ambassador, Inventor, Investor, Strategist, Student, and Coach? What percentage of your time are you spending within each role? If your answer is less than 80%, what is your plan to change that? If you subscribe to Glenn Horton's three roles of the CEO, have you defined what those three things are for you and how much of your time is spent there? If you follow Dan Barnett's concept of "Make or Break," do you own the organization's "Make and Break" down to the detail level? This means that the CEO should own the make or break and only the make or break down to the detail level. Dan in his life succeeded in taking four companies to number one in their marketplace. At Van de Kamps, it was freshness, at Juicy Juice, it was distribution, at Continental Brands, it was acquisition, and at Vistage International, it was chair recruitment. Do you own the make or break in your organization and are you involved in only the make or break down to the detail level?

Recently, I was making a presentation to a Vistage International group and one of the members, who happened to be a contractor, shared with me that he was working numerous hours and not making a lot of progress. During my presentation, he came to realize that he did a great job of building the company during the entrepreneurial phase, yet he needed a different skill set to get the company to the next level.

Similarly, I would ask you, if the next step in your organization is to get to a higher level what do you think the most important characteristics of that are? You may have intuitively known how to develop your business at the entrepreneurial stage, but taking your business to the next level may require professional management. Do you have that skill set? Are you willing to do that?

Or, is it time for you to consider hiring that person? As the Investor, it's your fiduciary responsibility to determine who the best person is for that and it may not be you. What realization have you come to?

One of my members once asked me if I would create and chair his board. And I said, "No."

Surprised, he asked me, "Why not?"

Very briefly I said, "I'm the wrong kind of guy to chair your board."

Thirty days later he came back to me and again asked, "What would it take for you to build a board for me?"

I thought for a minute and in my straightforward way I said, "The ability to fire you."

Again, with a surprised look on his face he said, "Well, what do you mean?"

I went on to explain, "My struggle with you is, if I'm going to be on a board, I'm going to expect accountability. Accountability starts at every seat in the organization. So, if you set the company out on a certain performance standard and you're not making those numbers, then as the Chairman of the Board, it's my responsibility to put somebody in that position who can achieve the results. That doesn't mean you don't get to keep ownership, but as a fiduciary of the business, we need to put the best person possible in that position." He hasn't hired me yet.

It's important to realize, none of this means you have to exit what you're doing. It's really just a matter of finding the right people and put them in the right seats to support you and your vision.

WHEN TO ARGUE WITH SUCCESS!

I have always said, "If you're getting what you want done, done, then keep doing what you're doing. If you're not getting what you want, then let's take a look at the model."

In your business, and in your life, are you getting what you want? Should you stick with your business model? Does it need to be changed?

As I shared before, Don McNeill at Digital Kitchen had a successful business providing creative services that combined digital imagery and live action for the film and commercial industries. Although already successful, he took a leap out of his current business model, and established a new model, *Team Disrupt*...and the rest is *True Blood, Transformers*, Nike, Target, and BMW history.

What is your "model" at home and in your organization...and is it working? Are you getting what you want out of your relationships, your business, and all aspects of your life? If you are, then just keep doing what you're doing. You've figured something out that most of us haven't. If you're not, I would urge you to take a look at the gaps in your life and start making adjustments.

What has always struck me, in visualizing the actions of my life, is an image of footprints in the sand. As you walk along in life, what you leave behind are imprints. My imprints are pretty clear to me. There isn't a time that I close my eyes and visualize my foot imprints in the sand that there isn't a small set of feet beside me.

What do you want your imprint to be—not what you think it's supposed to be, but what you really identify with and what you really want? Think back to your *ingoaltions*. And most importantly, who and what will get the "time of your life"?

CHAPTER SIX
LIVE AUTHENTICALLY

Many years ago, I heard the story of a guest that was walking through NASA headquarters in Washington D.C. when he met one of the NASA custodians in the hallway. Inquisitive, he asked the custodian what his job was. The custodian promptly replied, "To put men in space."

Now that's a custodian who truly understands the purpose of NASA, their culture, and his contribution within it! Think about it: if you dig a little bit deeper into this line of thought, doesn't a significant amount of the work NASA conducts in their test labs depend upon a clean and sterile environment? With this added awareness, it becomes clearly important that the custodian understands his contribution towards putting men into space and feels like a valued member of the NASA team.

GETTING CLEAR ON "CULTURE"

In his book *Leadership: Thinking, Being, Doing*, Lee Thayer says, "If you want to see the organization you deserve, look at the one you've got." In short, your organization is designed exactly the way it is to give you the results that you're getting. So, if you want something different, you need to come up with a different design, which speaks to the culture and structure of the organization.

At a hospital where I coach the leadership team, I heard that the head custodian talked to his team in terms of, "We are the environment that allows the physicians and the doctors to cure the patients. For all intents and purposes, we create the overall theater for allowing the healing work to be done." Here, the head custodian wasn't talking about cleaning, mopping the floor, or picking up trash. He was speaking to his team's purpose and inspiring them to truly feel and understand how they contribute to the organization and more globally, to the well-being of others.

Many companies try to copy remarkable cultures, with little success. Another example of an amazing culture that you are likely familiar with is Southwest Airlines. Numerous other airlines tried to copy Southwest Airlines' business plan-- Delta with Delta Connect, United Airlines with TED, and American Airlines with American Eagle. Southwest may have had a competitive advantage due to the fact that they only flew one type of airplane, the 737, and this helped with maintenance and training costs; however, their true success came along with the culture they live and breathe.

I heard Mike Milliken speak years ago where he said, companies that had access to technology won the last decade of the last century. Organizations that had access to capital won the first decade of *this* century. And those companies that will win the next decade of this generation, the one they're in now, will win the culture war.

Even when the competitor airlines copied other aspects of Southwest's success, what they never truly could get was the culture and the fact that every employee at Southwest knew their contributory role within the company. They knew that "we (Southwest as a whole) make money when our planes are in the air!" Living the culture, baggage handlers and flight attendants alike focused on turning planes around with lightning speed.

Have you ever flown on a Southwest flight? Upon exiting the plane, did you ever notice that the flight attendants immediately start to remove the trash and get things in order while you are exiting the plane, so as to assist with a speedy turn around? As a matter of fact, at Southwest, they refer to Delta as "Don't Ever Leave the Airport!" Additionally, have you ever noticed the contrast of how American Airlines flight attendants stand behind the cockpit, thanking you for flying "American" instead of simultaneously getting the plane ready for departure while thanking you?

Take a moment to think about it: How are you consistent or inconsistent within your culture?

It was Carole who first said to me, "Kids learn what's caught, not what's taught." I've found that this applies to both my personal and business life. One of the great examples of this, which also speaks to the point that more than 80% of our communication is nonverbal, is comparing the cultures of the United States Military.

I was working with a peer who had graduated from the United States Naval Academy, and we started a discussion around culture with a CEO. As part of this discussion, my co-worker explained, "We have a choice when we graduate from the Naval Academy. We can join the U.S. Marine Corp, or we can join the U.S. Navy. One of the differences between the Marines and the Navy is evidenced at mealtime. The culture of the Marines is that the officers eat in the mess hall, with the same food, in the same uniforms, and in the same way as the enlisted men. Whereas, in contrast, Navy Officers eat at white tablecloths with china and dress uniforms, separate from the enlisted men. These are two very successful organizations, with two entirely different cultures.

The CEO went on to say, "I believe more in the Marine culture." This was further evidenced by the fact that he had a cubicle just like everyone else in his organization. No one in the company had private offices. He was very proud of the fact that he was part of a "Marine-like culture." However, there was one important piece where he was incongruent within his stated culture. When it came to the company parking lot, there were only four parking spaces in front of the door and one of them was reserved for him, while everybody else parked in the adjacent parking lot. Through this inconsistent nonverbal communication, part of the clarity of culture was lost.

Jeff Mariola, the former President of Ambius and current CEO and Partner of Digital Brand Works, once shared that one of the things he observes when visiting a company is the greenery and plant life. If there is greenery in the reception area, he'll go back into the bowels of the organization and if they don't have greenery back there, he takes this as a mixed message with regard to their culture. Does a company that has inconsistent nonverbal communication, like the greenery test, treat their employees differently than they do their guests? Most likely, yes!

There are all types of subtle nonverbal communications that can give you away as to how you really do things. Do you act differently when there's a customer in the building? Do you have separate break rooms for executives and general employees? Do you have plants and greenery in your lobby and yet a sterile environment exists throughout the remainder of the building? It all comes down to those subtle messages and what they are meant to say.

HOW DO YOU DEFINE AND DEVELOP CULTURE?

There is no single process to defining and developing culture. There are so many companies who have developed successful cultures, and no two are alike.

General Electric (GE) is the perfect example of a very successful business, where the culture is very competitive and you're rewarded by getting promotions, more work, and longer hours. There's no confusion about what the culture is within the company. In a GE type of culture, rewards are based on individual competitiveness. If you're drafted into a team, it's typically because the team wants the top players. Edgar Papke, a globally recognized thought leader and expert in organizational alignment, uses a great team building analogy to describe a culture like GE's. As he explains, if you were to take the GE group on a teambuilding, river rafting expedition, it would be a race down the river!

Conversely, when you visit Disney, another very successful company and culture, it's all about the customers. Disney's culture is collaborative and focused on customer experience and satisfaction. For example, if you park in the Disney parking lot and have car trouble, they have people monitoring the parking lot to ensure, from the time you arrive until the time you leave, you have been in the "Magic Kingdom." Applying Papke's team building analogy, if you take the Disney group out on a teambuilding, river rafting expedition, you are going to send that group out on a boat where they can work together.

Starbucks is another very successful company with a distinct, employee-focused, culture. Starbucks employees are empowered to create their own schedules by working it out amongst the team at large. Their employee focus is present down to the level of determining what music is played in the store, with the employee of the day taking charge of the decision. A compensation program in a culture like Starbucks is going to be determined based on how the employees agree to apportion it. It's all about them. If you were to take Starbucks employees on Papke's teambuilding, river rafting expedition, the key would be to take them to the river, give them access to the boats and then let them decide how they want to proceed.

What often happens in developing our own cultures is that we state what we think our culture should be, but then we don't live it. Are you living your desired culture?

WHAT CULTURE ARE YOU CULTIVATING?

Cultivating a culture consistent with your actions can be tricky. You can meticulously design your culture from compensation, to physical organization, to customer interactions, but unless you live it, you'll never be truly successful. Take for instance Apple Inc.'s design culture. Steve Jobs saw buttons as a flawed design, and as a result, he designed Apple products without them. And perhaps more importantly, you never saw him wear buttons. By living the brand, as evidenced by only being seen in public, wearing T-shirts — no buttons — Steve Jobs cemented the importance of design to all of his constituents, customers, and as well as the employees and suppliers to Apple.

Getting a consistent message out is often the difficult part. Sometimes, the activities and rewards within your company may not be aligned to your culture and goals. In the case of one of my members, what she ultimately realized is that the fun and playful culture, as she was defining it within her company, was only about the employees. It wasn't congruent with the culture she put forth with the company's suppliers, investors, or customers.

Your culture is experiential for your employees, suppliers, and customers, and every one of them needs to know exactly what to expect when you're handling them.

Any inconsistencies start to diminish the message. Take for example United Airlines slogan, "Come fly the friendly skies!" That slogan became such a joke, because it wasn't carried through to your experience on the plane. Your culture is experiential for your employees, suppliers, and customers, and every one of them needs to know exactly what to expect when you're handling them.

It's also important to remember as I've said before, more than 80% of communication, including culture, is nonverbal. Illustrating this point, one of my members who is the president of a nationally-recognized, award-winning company, shared with me, "Bob, I have an open door policy." In truth, he does; however, the problem is nobody's walking through it! So our challenge was finding out where the message was getting filtered and who was telling his employees that they couldn't come in. After some brief investigation, the source became apparent.

While sharing a story about a recent interaction, my member explained that an employee came into his office with an idea and that he, the vice president, and the director approved. Curious, I asked, "What would happen if the vice president did not agree with the director? Would that idea have ever seen the light of day?"

As it turns out, his answer was, "Not likely." So again, he had an open door policy, but the problem is nobody's walking through the "open door" unless they think what they have to say fits the criteria of approval. Again, he's talking about the culture, but he hasn't taken actions to really affirm it. The words, "open door policy," don't match the actions at every level of the organization. And, as leader of the organization, he was being watched for these signals.

WHAT CULTURE ARE YOU CULTIVATING ON THE HOME FRONT?

The same considerations are true when it comes to establishing family culture. What's your family culture? Is it collaborative? If you are parents, are you established as the experts? Or, is it an open culture? Applying Edgar Papke's teambuilding analogy one more time, if your family was going down the river, is it a competition? Are you doing it together? Or, do you allow everyone in the family to decide how they're going to go down the river?

What happens when you have a child that's a real competitor, and yet you have another child who isn't? Do you force competition? How do you align that story? That goes back to, how do you deal with an introvert in an extroverted society? How do you deal with three members of the family who are extroverts and one who is an introvert? Do you communicate to that child that they're not all right? That they don't fit into the "family culture"?

I came from a competitive family. In contrast, Carole's family wasn't the least bit competitive. But the one thing we all had in common was that we all loved sports. Sports were a natural attraction for everyone in the family, with the exception of Jenny, who hated anything to do with a ball.

When Jenny was twelve, she was preparing for her bat mitzvah and the cantor said to us, "Do you know that Jenny has perfect pitch?" Well, to me, perfect pitch is a 90 mile per hour fast ball. All joking aside, I'm glad that we were made aware of her talent because Jenny then went on to excel at choir and drama. One of the highlight of Jenny's adolescent years was when she got the lead role in her camp play.

In one instance, I went with Jenny to a class they were teaching around art history in Italy because Jenny and her choir were planning on going to Italy to sing. And, as the teacher tied art history into the history and government of Italy, I sat there spellbound.

My camp experience, as well as my son's experience, was centered on athletics. But it came clear to me that Jenny loved her camp experience just as much; it was just different than ours. This experience really opened up my eyes to really

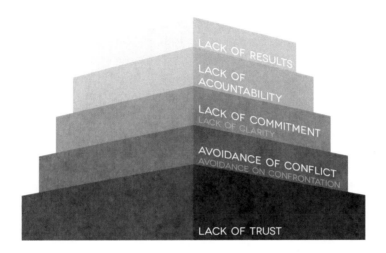

understand that she got the same thing from her choir that I did from my sports—how to participate in a group, be a member of a team, and put on a production.

Jenny had found her own path. And as it turned out, her experience expanded our family culture in amazing and unanticipated ways.

So again, if your customers are your children, spouses, or significant others, aren't they your most important customers? Are you putting the same focus on developing the right culture in your family as you are your business? And, are you willing to accept somebody else's path other than your own?

CREATING AN ACCOUNTABILITY CULTURE

I often refer to Patrick Lencioni's *Five Dysfunctions of a Team* and his pyramid of Absence of Trust, Fear of Conflict, Lack of Commitment, Avoidance of Accountability, and Inattention to Results.

As Patrick Lencioni teaches us, and as I have learned from my experiences, if we are not getting the results we want, it's time to look under the covers. To go anywhere in a business or in any relationship, there has to be a foundation of trust. Once trust is established, we can have healthy confrontation (as clearly evidenced in the functional relationship between Lincoln and Seward). Once voices have been heard, we can reach commitment and clarity. Then we can assign accountability. If all these steps are in place, dysfunction becomes function that gives us the best chance to achieve the results we want.

I once performed an offsite coaching session for a company, and during our session, we did a lot of work around trust, as it fits into the *Five Dysfunctions of a Team*. I remember being impressed with how one of the managers was open and transparent about some of the things that were going wrong in the field. It was a really good, healthy conversation. However, I later learned that the manager's candor was reported back to his boss after our meeting. Surprisingly, the boss's response was, "Don't ever do that again. Don't talk about the mistakes we're making in the field." Here they were trying to build an open culture, where they could talk about challenges in order to try to fix them, and the boss was a saboteur. It only takes one.

When I was asked to become president of Milgram Kagan, the chairman, Bill Hellman, and I had come to an agreement. As I was meeting with his number two executive to go over the details of the contract, just before I signed it, he said to me, "Bobby, I just want you to know, we are really happy with the senior team that's at the company."

Not quite clear about his intention I asked, "What are you trying to tell me?"

And he reiterated, "Well, we just really like the team that's in place."

After asking for clarification for a third time, and receiving a similar answer, I stood up, shook his hand and said, "Clarence, thank you very much. Just tell Bill I'm not going to move forward with this."

Early Monday morning, I received a call from Bill, asking me, "What the hell happened?" And I repeated the conversation to him. He said, "Bobby, if you go in next Monday morning and you fire the entire senior team, that's your choice!"

I was asked to coach a vice president of sales and as I was deciding if I wanted to or not, the owner of the company came in and joined my interview. The goal for the vice president of sales was to expand sales both domestically and internationally and he would have to add to his team. I asked, "Who owned hiring the new sales associates?" The owner said that the vice president of sales would hire the team but the owner would have final say. I asked the owner why, and he responded by saying that he wanted to make sure that the new hires fit the company culture. I asked how long the vice president of sales had worked for him and the response was twenty years. I told the owner I would not take the assignment unless the vice president of sales had the final decision making authority for his team. If he didn't own "his team" how could we hold him accountable for the result? Did the owner want to protect the culture or exert his control?

Establishing an *accountability culture* comes down to just that—account-ability. How are decisions made? Who owns the decisions? Does the budget win? Does performance win? What are the hard measures that you're holding others or yourself accountable to? That can be a really tough edge.

Whenever I start a meeting I say, "I'm going to start at eight o'clock." And I start at eight o'clock. The question often arises, do I want to be held account-able to do what I said I would do, when I said I would do it, or am I going to honor the people who are invariably late? And if I honor the people that are late, what message am I sending about respecting time, and what am I saying about me? Also, when we call a break, I don't say, "Come back in ten min-utes." I say, "I'm going to start again in ten minutes." I start whether everyone is back in the room or not. However, if I let people drift back in and I don't start when I say I'm going to start, I'm creating a grey area around sticking to my word. Ultimately, there's only one person I can hold accountable—*myself*.

Holding yourself accountable to your own word allows people to rely upon you. I don't know about you, but I would much rather work for some-one and be with someone in a family who I know what I'm going to get. If I have to go to work or come home to a different person each day and figure out whom I'm dealing with, now that's a difficult situation to live with.

I once had an appointment with the owner of a business. He walked into our appointment about twenty minutes late and in a fairly loud voice pro-claimed, "Traffic on the Kennedy held me up." My response to actions like this is, "Are you going to create an accountability culture or an excuse cul-ture?" If you're coming in with the excuse of why you're late, the next person in your company is going to come in with their own brand of excuse that they had to walk the dog. And the next person is going to come in with their excuse that there was a line when they had to drop off the dry cleaning.

What is your culture around accountability? Do you do what you say you will do? Or, do you and others in your company just meander in, and get to work on your own time frames? Attendance might not be important to you, but again, what's your culture and are you consistent with that? People—chil-dren, employees, spouses—need consistency. If you are continuously incon-sistent, then people don't know how to behave.

As a leader, your role is to absorb any stress, not to bring extra stress to the organization or family. Accountability, if done right, should relieve stress, because it's clear communication around established expectations. You will find, strong people gravitate towards accountability, whereas weak people are going to hide from it.

Don't you want good people who are comfortable being held accountable in your business, in your family and in your life? People who want to be part of an *accountability culture*?

YOUR CULTURE = YOUR LIFE

It's amazing to me how many people live with so much pain and lack of joy because they are not living life with authenticity, as their normal self. They can't or won't live "all-in" out of fear of something.

- "I can't speak my truth to the boss."
- "I don't think the company does what it says it will."
- "I have been promised a raise for months."

Why do we stay in dysfunctional relationships—business or personal? Ever heard the story of a person, staying in a pit with a poisonous snake hissing at their ankles? As they start to climb out, half way up they hear a tiger roaring, and they crawl back into the hole with the snake and almost certain death. What is the story they are telling themselves?

Are you getting the results you want? If not, is it about a lack of trust in some of your key relationships? Are you able to have confrontational, face-to-face conversations with key relationships? Do you speak with clarity? Are you willing to hold yourself accountable, and if you're not getting the results you want, have the courage to make changes? Are you living life authentically to your values?

Live your culture and your life authentically, whatever that is to you. You'll be amazed at how it will influence other people.

CHAPTER SEVEN

STAND UNDER YOUR OWN ARCH

It is said that the engineers who built the great structures and temples of ancient Rome stood accountable for their work by literally standing within the archways as the capstones were put into place. Now that's what I call being held accountable!

During my tenure with Vistage International, people have often asked me, "What makes a successful Vistage International Chair?" My response back to them is, "It's the same two characteristics you see if you look at successful people—they have a passion for what they're doing and they hold themselves accountable." At times, my Vistage International groups have gone so far as to ask me to hold them accountable and my response is always the same: "I can't hold anyone accountable but myself!" I can merely remind them of what they asked to be held accountable to.

It's always interesting to me that people, who like to collaborate with others, can confuse the concept of collaboration with someone who has to own authority and responsibility. You can meet as a team and then let democracy decide if you're going to have five of the team members govern, but you still have to be accountable for the action of choosing how the team should be governed. I can't tell you how many times I've heard "We're accountable" in an organization. There is no such thing as "we" accountability. Its okay to collaborate and get input, but someone has to own "it."

WHAT'S BEHIND AN AVERSION TO BE HELD ACCOUNTABLE?

I think for many people it goes back to the stress driver, "I'm not good enough" or "I don't trust my decision." And again, the higher up you go in an organization, you have to predict or make decisions about the future. Logically, the only way you can get real statistical support is to go back into the past to see what worked and what didn't. Looking backward may feel safe; however, it is not a precursor to the future.

During the economic downturn that started in 2008, why did some manufacturing companies invest in new equipment that made their facilities more efficient, while others were holding onto their cash? Why were some companies being frugal with their cash while others were increasing their marketing budgets? Why did some companies pursue new markets in South and Central America while others were reducing overhead? These are the kinds of decisions that leaders must be making at all times. Returning to what Jack Welch said, "If the rate of change outside your business is faster than the rate of change inside your business, you lose!"

As I talked about previously, when I was in the shoe business, I used to say that every year the buyers made a perfect buy for last year. If we were short of trendy blue shoes in the present year, the following year the buyer would buy more blue shoes. However, a real problem arose with this approach, as every year there would be a new blue, or other color trend. Predicting the future is not an exact science.

Dr. Gerry Faust once said, "A company's balance sheet is an indicator of the present value of the past performance of a company." It is true that sometimes past performance is an indicator of future performance, yet, it is important to keep in mind that there are a myriad of other influential factors at work, one of the most important being *your actions*.

In the spring of 2011, President Obama had a very difficult decision to make surrounding the raid to try and capture or kill the former leader of al-Qaeda, Osama Bin Laden. Looking back into history and the two previous Democratic administrations of Presidents Carter and Clinton, President Obama could have easily made a decision to use a drone attack, rather than a helicopter incursion. Some people believe that the helicopters that went down in the Iranian desert during the Iranian hostage crisis cost Jimmy Carter the second term to his presidency. President Clinton also almost lost his presidency due to the downing of two Black Hawk helicopters in The Battle of Mogadishu, more commonly known as "Black Hawk Down." With two past unsuccessful helicopter raids in presidential history, the easy decision for President Obama would have been a drone strike and not risking the lives of the Seals or having the helicopters shot down. However, he also knew that a drone attack might never prove whether Osama Bin Laden had been successfully taken care of. I call that accountable leadership.

How about you? Are you willing to be wrong and make the decisions on your best understanding of what's going on out in the world? Or are you dead set on basing all of your decisions around what has happened in the past, just to be certain you are "right." At the end of the day, the leader must weigh all the factors, make sure he or she has considered all the options, the cause and effect of the decision and then act.

WITHOUT FAILURE, NOTHING MOVES FORWARD

Most organizations have a tendency to focus on results to define their success, rather than developing healthy approaches to risk and failure. One of the most important concepts to remember surrounding growth is, "Without failure, nothing moves forward." …And, my definition of risk is not trying!

As Dr. Rick Eigenbrod, a clinical psychologist with a focus on organizational behavior and leadership says, "We don't grow as individuals from positive events. Most of our growth comes from difficult times." This is related to the J-Curve we'll be discussing later on.

As mentioned previously, *Harvard Business Review* ran an article titled, "The CEO's Role in Business Model Reinvention." The article stated that companies make a mistake by focusing performance rewards on annual financial performances. Instead, they suggested that someone should be rewarded for annual results, someone should be rewarded for stopping the company from doing things (so you could get rid of legacy programs that ceased adding value), and someone should get paid for failing to enable continuous innovation.

I was conducting a one-on-one coaching session while driving to a meeting with a senior executive at an online marketing company. Up until this point, the executive had worked for large companies or equity companies that focused on short-term, monthly, and annual financial goals, while his new company was focused on making the right investments to build strong infrastructure to insure long-term growth.

As our session unfolded, it surfaced that he was frustrated about having decided to work for an entrepreneurial business, where inside that entrepreneurial business they weren't making money and they were experiencing a negative cash flow. He wanted to quickly "fix it" in the short-term, whereas the owner of the company was telling him to keep his eyes on the long-term target of building enterprise value. It's very interesting to watch this executive who, in his own mind, is failing right now, but at the same time, is doing exactly what the owner is supportive of—spending some money on marketing, introducing some new products, hiring some new staff, and preparing the business for the future. He's making a lot of the right decisions, and I believe that ultimately, he'll be rewarded but right now, it's a very difficult place for him.

In my mind, trust is doing what you said you would do, when you said you would do it, period.

How do you define failure? As I stated before, I define failure as not trying. I can't always determine the outcome, but at the end of the day, I can only do the best I can do. Continually going back into the past will only serve to drive yourself crazy over the things you did wrong. Instead, learn from them. Someone once said to me, "The biggest waste of time in the world is wishing for a better past." What story do you tell yourself about failure and success?

On October 14, 2012, Austrian daredevil Felix Baumgartner ascended in a helium-filled balloon to the edge of the atmosphere and then did a free-fall jump 128,100 feet back to Earth, breaking the sound barrier. I would think he defined risk as "not going."

THE FUNDAMENTALS OF ACCOUNTABILITY

Trust

As you can tell, I really respect the work of Patrick Lencioni, and most especially his book *The Five Dysfunctions of a Team*. One of the foundational pieces of this book stems from how different individuals view trust.

How do you interpret trust? In my mind, trust is doing what you said you would do, when you said you would do it, period.

Earlier in the book, we briefly discussed what an accountability culture is and why you would want to have one. The bottom line is, if you don't have an accountability culture, it's likely because somewhere along the way you've eroded trust by not meeting your agreements.

The foundation of any successful family or business is *trust*. And trust begins with honesty. In his seminars, Balaji Krishnamurthy teaches three levels of honesty. The first is, "Tell the truth, and don't steal." The second is, "Always do what you said you would do." The third level is, "Always speak your truth."

Speaking to this trust issue, what happens in your own relationships professionally and personally when a trust has been violated? How can you try to get trust back and what do you carry with you when you live outside of or violate your own moral compass or personal agreements? In my experience, whenever trust is violated it carries a pretty big weight.

At its foundation, it comes down to asking yourself, "Do I trust you enough that I can have an honest relationship and tell you what I think, or am I mincing my words, am I choosing not to speak?" And, do I trust myself enough to know my motivation is based on positive intent.

Revisiting Susan Scott's book, *Fierce Conversations*, if you're not willing to have the conversation, why is that? Is it that you don't trust the relationship? Or is it that you don't trust how you're going to feel? If you withhold your experiences, what you're really trying to do is protect yourself and you've moved out of service of helping the other person.

If you have a boss and you think he only wants you to tell him what he wants to hear and you can't speak your truth—well, first of all, why would you want to work for a boss like that? Why would you want to be in an environment like that? And, how dysfunctional is that organizationally? If you're going to build a world-class organization, does the senior team trust each other and do you have meetings and interchanges where people are willing to speak their truth? Do you have a family? If so, are your children able to speak their truth? Are the people surrounding you respectfully given their voice?"

I sometimes think the most powerful voice in a group of people (business, family, or otherwise) that are all saying, "We should go in one direction," is the quiet voice that comes up from the table and says, "Guys, I hear you all, but maybe we should consider this."

I tell people who join Vistage International that it is the best place to come to get your answers questioned, versus your questions answered. By telling the group about what you are doing and then receiving fifteen other points of view, you can feel confident that you have thought of most everything. And, at the end of the day, you still own that decision.

Abraham Lincoln was an excellent example of this concept. He let everyone in his cabinet express themselves. Then, having been heard, they were able to go out as a united front and clearly express the delivery of the Emancipation Proclamation.

This is beautifully depicted in Spielberg's movie, *Lincoln*. President Lincoln and Seward are arguing. Seward wants Lincoln to end the Civil War because thousands of American citizens are dying on both sides of the battle every day. Lincoln understands that if he ends the war and the South returns to the union, he will never have enough votes to pass the 13th Amendment. After a heated and lengthy dispute, Lincoln, bangs the table and states, "I am the President. We are going to pass the 13th Amendment!" After that has been clearly decided, Seward calmly turns to the team and says, "Let's go get the votes!" Everyone was heard, however, President Lincoln owned the final decision.

It's as we talked about before with regard to watching the movie *A Beautiful Mind*; we see things through our own filters making it easy to convince ourselves why we're right. In contrast, having open dialogue and feedback is really the healthiest approach.

Confrontation (a.k.a. Carefrontation)

The next level up from trust is the willingness to have confrontation, or as we playfully say in Vistage International, *carefrontation*. I care enough about you to have an honest conversation with you. It's interesting that in American society, confrontation has a negative connotation. However, if you go back to the Latin root, all confront means is "with face." It all boils down to, "Do I trust our relationship, and do I trust myself enough that I am willing to have those hard, fierce conversations?"

The goal of the fierce conversation is not to create the change, but for you to speak your truth. The only time I have seen someone's behavior change towards me is after I changed my behavior to them.

Revisiting what Susan Scott stated in *Fierce Conversations*, "Marriages and businesses go bad slowly and then quickly due to conversations we're not willing to have." It all comes down to, "I care enough about you, and I care enough about our relationship to trust enough to be willing to confront you," which is where *carefrontation* comes from.

What are the *carefrontations* that you are not having in your life?

Clarity and Commitment

After *carefrontation*, Lencioni's next step is *commitment*. However, in my experience, you can't get to commitment without *clarity*. When I speak of clarity, I'm talking about getting clear on what you're doing, what the expectations are, and who owns the decisions.

I believe it is important that any meeting establish two things: first, what is the objective? Sometimes this can just be an exchange of ideas and other times the end result is to make a decision. Secondly, if a decision needs to be made, who owns the decision? If I have a direct report and the decision is theirs, then I know my role is to be an advisor, even though I might be above them on an organizational chart.

In my experience, clarity is usually avoided and leaders speak in generalities or vaguely, because they don't want to have to deal with the negative consequences if someone doesn't do what they said they would be accountable for. Interestingly, the rest of the leadership team knows what action should be taken and is typically aware of the negative impact the action has throughout the culture of the company or the disciplinary structure at home.

Transparency in Today's World

Patrick Lencioni wrote another book called *Getting Naked*, which is written from a consultant's point of view about the ability to be totally open and just speak the truth—in essence, to be *transparent*. Transparency is communicating, "This is what I feel. I'm open to just saying what I believe." In large part, transparency as a leader is being vulnerable. It may be that you don't have all the answers and are open to working things out collaboratively.

A great example of this comes from Jim Collins' book, *Good to Great*. The president of Wells Fargo knew that deregulation was coming, he just wasn't sure of the decisions that he would have to face. His strategic answer was to hire the brightest minds that he could. When deregulation came they were positioned with the best intellectual capital, made more "good decisions" and separated themselves from their competition.

On a family basis, so many people are brought up to not cry in front of your children, or to not show weakness. What happens when they're grown up and they feel weak and they want to cry? Have they now been told that that is bad? I think that we, as parents and leaders, do a great service to our kids and our employees when we share we're not one hundred percent certain where we're going or how we are going to get there. However, it's important to be willing to own the decision, and be positive that we're going to work it out. Courage isn't about not being afraid. Courage is doing "it" even when you are afraid.

I've made it a habit to share my feelings, fears and thoughts with my kids. If they don't see me in touch with my feelings or that I have fears, what are

In order to be successful in this day and age, the whole person has to show up in a relationship, business and personal alike.

they going to think later in life when they have fears or are afraid? I think the biggest change in my relationship with Jenny was when she was sixteen and we had a verbal knockdown, drag out disagreement. It was a Saturday night and I had reached a point where I had enough and I said, "That's it, Jenny, you're not going out tonight!" She immediately responded by running up the stairs and slamming her door. And then, much to my anger, the front door slammed, and she went out.

Fortunately for me, I had a live-in therapist. Carole asked me, "What are you going to do next?"

I promptly responded, "You mean, after I kill her?"

I'd like to think the next hour and a half was a dialogue, but it was really a monologue of Carole talking to *me* about what I was trying to accomplish with Jenny. About two hours later, Jenny called back and asked Carole, "Is it safe to come home?"

I heard Carole calmly say, "Yes."

When Jenny arrived home, I followed her up the stairs and she climbed into bed. I sat on the foot of her bed and I said, "Honey, I want to thank you for tonight." I said, "All I want to do is to keep you safe and help you grow up to be the woman you want to be. And what you taught me tonight is that I can't do that anymore. And so, from this moment forward, you have one rule, and that is, if you're not going to sleep in your bed, call your mother."

What did Jenny want? Jenny just wanted to be treated like an adult. What did I want? I wanted her to be an adult, and yet, I was treating her like a child. When I gave her what she wanted—to be an adult—that was the beginning of the change of our relationship. It was a big risk for me, but at sixteen, she was ready to make those kinds of decisions. I don't think we've had a cross word since.

In the early stages of my relationship with Carole, I brought into the relationship that I was a fraud and she brought into the relationship that she couldn't trust. And until we were able to talk about those things and be open and transparent, we really had no chance of building a meaningful relationship.

What insecurities, weaknesses, or concerns are you hiding within your family or organization?

The Industrial Revolution is over: where you go to work at nine o'clock and you leave your personal life behind and then at five o'clock you can become a person again. In order to be successful in this day and age, the whole person has to show up in a relationship, business and personal alike.

I recently conducted a senior team meeting at a company and one of the items on the agenda was the president's "stay up at night" list. This list was comprised of the things that he wanted to make sure he was in line with his senior team on. Before we started his portion of the meeting, I suggested we talk about everyone's "stay up at night" list. We went around the table and one of the vice presidents just started crying. What was keeping her up at night was that it was budget time and she was overwhelmed. As it turned out, her husband traveled Monday through Friday. So, when she gets home from work, she then has to work with her kids with their homework and take care of other family responsibilities, and she was just overwhelmed. Luckily, in their company culture, it was okay for her to express the personal side to her life, providing the opportunity to overlap the conversation into what the contributing stresses were within the organization. And, although the amount of work couldn't be reduced, we were able to collectively strategize how to relieve some of the stress that was being placed on her within the organization.

The culture within the company made it okay for this Vice President to share her challenges with balancing her demands at home with her demands at work. The beauty of this team is that she was supported and she was able to speak her truth. She was able to release much of her pressure, enabling her to better focus on the job at hand.

The bottom line is that the only way to create transparency is to be transparent. The question is, are you willing?

What do you really want? Is your current behavior getting you what you want? Are you carrying around stuff that you're not cleaning up? That's what it's really about. Can you be your authentic self? Do people around you allow for transparency? If you believe that the conversation is the relationship, what's the conversation you're not having?

A Vistage International member of mine loved his wife and she loved him; however, they were on a path of separating in their marriage and were not dealing with their issues. During one of our meetings, I asked him what his vision for the future was. In response, he shared that his vision was for he and his wife to retire in Florida so that they could spend time together and walk on the beach. After identifying that if they kept behaving the way they were behaving that wasn't going to happen, he sat down with his wife. He shared his vision for their life together and his concern that with their current behavior it wasn't going to work out. As it turns out, his wife wanted the same thing, but they just needed to have an open, transparent conversation to realize it. Even though they lost their direction for a little bit, they are now working together towards the same goal and vision.

In another case, one of my members said his biggest goal for the next year was to have a more intimate relationship with his wife. The next month he was offered to sit on the international board of his trade association. I asked him what he was going to do and he said, "I'm going to accept it."

I said, "Let me ask you a question. How does that create a more intimate relationship with your wife?"

What he came to realize is his image, and the way he was perceived in his business, was more important. As a result, he had a transparent conversation with his wife, sharing with her that he needed to take the position and that he wasn't going to be home as much as he used to be. She thanked him for being open and honest. Now, she knew what she needed to do to fill her time and knew not to wait and expect it from him. That wouldn't work for me in my relationship with my wife, but it worked for them.

ACCOUNTABLE RESULTS

All results start with gaining clarity around the results you want. Whether it's a business or a family result, even if you have an agreement on the result, sometimes you're not clear on it. If that's the case, take the time to go back down into the *Five Dysfunctions* cycle of trust, confrontation, clarity, commitment, accountability, and finally, results. Are you clear at every level?

In our family, Carole and I have rarely had to break ties. However, it was clear if the issue was about the kids, she got the final say. She allowed me to air my thoughts and it may have, at times, changed her decision. Yet, we were clear it was her decision. While at the same time, I owned the financial decisions, and at times, did change my decision after her council. I hear a lot in business about "we own the decision" or worse "the boss owns all the decisions." Make sure there is accountability and clarity at every level. Also, put a system in place that rewards the results that were outlined and an appropriate series of consequences for non-performance.

Once you get really clear and specific, you can then measure what needs to be done to get the desired results. If the new product development team isn't getting you the new products in time, then how do you have that conversation? It's about being open, piecing things together, and not blaming. Strive to have robust, perhaps even *carefrontational* conversations around how to reach your results.

Family-wise, your goal may be to have more money in the bank at the end of the year than you did at the end of the previous year. The key is to be clear on what your goal is, trust each other enough to have whatever tough conversations need to happen, and to own the process that will get you there.

When I started my career, my goal was that I would control my schedule by the time I was twenty-nine years old. I wanted to be at my kid's Little League games, concerts, plays—in short, everything they took part in while growing up. By identifying and quantifying my goal, I was able to make clear career decisions that fit into my life goal.

As a matter of fact, today, when I coach young people starting their career, I suggest to them that they define their life and let their career fit that, not the other way around. I recently made that suggestion to a fifty-year-old that was in the financial market arena, and he said that he wished someone had suggested that to him when he started out. He made career decisions where, when he looked back, he wished he had made other choices.

Take a moment to stop and consider…what decisions are you making? If you haven't already, it's time to get really clear on what decisions and actions support your ultimate goal; because once the kids are grown, you don't get a do-over.

HOLDING YOURSELF ACCOUNTABLE TO WHAT YOU WANT

Are you getting what you want? Remember Goldsmith's quote that I shared with you earlier—"What got you here won't get you there." Have you clearly defined what you want for you, your family and your business? What changes need to be made to get it there?

In the Introduction I asked you to contemplate the following questions:

- Are you on a path to the life you want to live?
- Do you have joy in your life?
- Are you living a life of significance?
- Are you living a life in alignment with who you are?
- Are you living somebody else's life?

If you're not getting what you want, it's time to step up and start holding yourself accountable to your own life. It's time to take ownership for building trust organizationally and personally, for being willing to confront and have those hard conversations. Don't be afraid to get clear. Don't be afraid to take personal accountability so you can get the results you want in all aspects of your life.

I hear a lot people blaming their parents for their lot in life. I believe that all of our parents did the best they could. Sometimes that might not have been great parenting. Yet, I have seen people come from those situations, claim their lives, and take responsibility for themselves, while other siblings live as victims. Victims are never accountable. It's always somebody else's fault. They just suck the wind out of anything, because they're not willing to be accountable for it.

My maternal grandfather died broke and my father died broke. So, initially, my story was that I was going to die broke. One day, I said this to my coach, and he smiled at me and said, "That's convenient. So, if you don't make it in life you've got your excuse that it's because of genetics?" From that moment on, I realized just how ridiculousness the story I had been telling myself was. Luckily, I had done enough personal work to be able to laugh at myself, but that was my story. I was the victim of poor financial genes.

So what's the story you tell yourself about that?

Growth is scary. But I think what's more scary is staying where you are and getting the results you're getting. Take a moment to think about your approach to growth and life in general. How do you define risk? How do you define failure? How do you define success? Are you willing to take the challenge and hold yourself accountable?

Going back to the great structures of ancient Rome, I know I could stand under my own arch. Could you?

CHAPTER EIGHT

BE, DO, AND BRING MORE

This concept of "our biggest strengths are our biggest weaknesses"—what does it really mean?

Sometimes, the best wisdom doesn't come from an E.E. Cummings quote. As Jack Handey, an American writer and cast member of the late night television show *Saturday Night Live*, famous for his *Deep Thoughts* comedy sketches once wrote, "If you think a weakness can be turned into a strength, I hate to tell you this, but that's another weakness."

My protective strategy—one that I have often misperceived as a strength—is *over-explanation.* On one occasion, Michael asked me what business Curt, one of my Vistage International members, was in. I started telling him about how Curt had gotten into the business, what his parents did, and all of the details surrounding his professional path. At one point, I finally noticed that Michael was sitting across from me with sort of a tuned-out posture and a glazed look in his eyes.

Halting myself in my tracks, I said, "Mike, ask me your question again."

He briefly restated, "What business is Curt in?"

This time I simply responded, "The lumber business."

With a slight smile, he said, "Thank you." I realized I was going through an over-explained, overly-detailed story when two words would have sufficed to answer what business Curt was in. With patience, and not just a little bit of good humor, Michael had just sat there nicely and let me go on!

Typically, throughout our schooling and early professional careers, our teachers or mentors focus us on developing our weaknesses, in essence strengthening them. And although I do believe there is some value to this, I believe there is more value to honing in on our strengths directly. Think about it, wouldn't you be best served by working on and really building your strengths, surrounding yourself with people whose competencies better support yours?

My wife, Carole, is learning this as Chair of her committee of Psychological Services of our *A Giving Heart Foundation*. Carole understands the psychological needs of her clients, but having somebody who can really take those thoughts and put it into a business plan so that it gets executed is invaluable. It's no different than my relationship with my writer for this book, Rachel Kowalski. I could probably write a book, but after reading chapter one, you would have to skip to the fourth paragraph in chapter seven, just to follow me! The question I had to ask myself was, would it have served me to really work on my writing skills at this time, or was I better served to pair with somebody who could write it well for me? Obviously, I chose the latter.

We see this "strengths-weakness" challenge arise in our schools all the time. As a society, we're constantly pushing our kids to succeed. Yet, when a child comes through who is wildly talented in a creative sense, and has difficulty developing the non-creative parts of his or her brain, the typical academic structure doesn't adequately support their growth. Instead, they focus on building up creative children in their areas of weakness, rather than focusing on nurturing their real skill set.

In a professional sense, I can't tell you how many times someone has joined one of my Vistage International groups, where they discover someone else in the group is far more proficient than they are in financing or marketing and, instead of asking for help, they beat themselves up over not having that skill.

Have you ever found yourself in this situation? If so, why are you not willing to honor the skills that you bring to the table? Why are you compelled to diminish what you do, and project out the strengths of others? What we really need to do is start working to bring all of our skills to the table!

During one of my group sessions, I asked people to do an exercise around their heroes, and what made them heroic. Surprisingly, it was easy for everyone to come up with what they viewed as heroic in other people and what actions were heroic. However, when I followed up by asking them when they were a hero or had done something heroic, they struggled answering. In turn, almost everyone could provide examples to each other of when they were heroes.

There is an executive in one of my groups whose niece is a special needs person. She was born unable to walk and she has a wonderful spirit. During one of our meetings, he shared how he and his niece would be in a shopping center and he'd be wheeling her around and how they would have the best of times together. In response, others in the group were telling him that what he did with his niece was heroic. However, he didn't think so; instead, he felt his time spent with his niece was just the natural thing to do.

Why do we push away these things that are acts of kindness and struggle with the definition of heroism in our own lives?

> Creative and divergent thinking is also invaluable professionally when it's applied at the right times and in the right positions. The key is to focus on what people are good at and allow them to do it.

RECOGNIZING GENIUS

The first time I was made aware of the concept of *recognizing genius* was in the *Journal of the Royal Society of Medicine* article that I mentioned earlier, where genius was defined as "divergent thinking." That, to me, is a much more meaningful aspect of genius than the typical discussions around IQ.

As you may recall, the study revolved around a group of kindergarteners, where 98 percent of them were at a genius level of divergent thinking. Five years later that genius had already dropped to 50 percent and five years beyond that, the number had dropped even more. I strongly believe this drop occurs because we teach people how to do tasks and work in a box, hindering creativity.

As a Little League coach, I always wondered why it always drove me crazy watching other coaches who would line up all of their seven to nine-year-old kids to hit ground balls to them one at a time. Essentially, they would have twelve kids standing around watching each other eventually hit balls. That's a recipe for disaster with kids. They get bored!

So, how do you keep everyone active and participating? My solution was to approach the National Honor Society at the local high school and enlist honor students who were looking for points to come and be my assistant coaches. I also simultaneously enlisted the participation of the parents, so that there were enough leaders out on the field with the kids to keep them active. A little creative and divergent thinking served to keep all of my Little League players active, while also fulfilling the needs and desires of honor students and parents—that's what I call a win-win-win!

Creative and divergent thinking is also invaluable professionally when it's applied at the right times and in the right positions. The key is to focus on what people are good at and allow them to do it.

For example, Ted Williams was arguably the best baseball hitter who ever lived. In fact, because of his hitting prowess he earned the nicknames, "The Splendid Splinter," "Teddy Ballgame," and "The Greatest Hitter Who Ever Lived." However, all that said, he was not a particularly good coach.

In another instance, take Tiger Woods' golf-swing coaches. None of them would ever beat him on the golf course, but they're certainly better at breaking down the science of the swing and helping get Tiger where he wants to go.

Take a moment to observe your own life—organizationally and in your family, do you honor the genius of those around you? Or, do you continue to be an "enemy"?

RAISING YOUR EMOTIONAL INTELLIGENCE

Learning about the concept of emotional intelligence (EQ) has been truly enlightening for me. I always liked to point out that my lowest numerical score, when compared against the business people who were in the same space as me, was impulse control.

Whenever we hear our numerical score, we tend to attach a plus or minus, good or bad, rather than "it just IS." In fact, all my score means is that my impulse control is lower than the people who I'm compared with. That's neither good nor bad. What's important is that I understand it and am aware of when my lack of impulse control serves me really well, and when it gets in my way.

For example, my lack of impulse control serves me and others well if there is an accident. In a case like this, I can focus on and quickly decide what needs to be done. Conversely, when a decision requires more thought I might not have the patience to seek all the possible options. Emotional intelligence, in my case, is getting clear and understanding when my lack of impulse control is a strength and when it is a weakness.

My personal experience is that all of the people that I coach, whether they're in one of my key groups, CEO groups, or outside of Vistage International, are more than capable of doing the job that they are hired to do. It's not their capabilities that hold them back from being successful, rather two other significant factors. Number one is culture and number two is their own EQ.

Up until recently, experts used to think that IQ could not be improved over life; however, now it is thought that it can be improved incrementally. In sharp contrast, Jim Liautaud, Founder and Chairman at the Liautaud Institute, conducted studies that show EQ can be improved by 15 percent over a lifetime.

The original study of emotional intelligence was done with a group of children. Control groups were offered a scoop of ice cream. If they could wait,

---

As Lao Tzu once said, "Knowing others is wisdom, knowing yourself is enlightenment."

---

they could have two scoops. Roughly a third of the kids took the one scoop immediately and another third tried to wait for the second but succumbed before the allotted time. The third group was able to wait for the second scoop. By a wide margin, those kids who were able to defer gratification did better in school, in life, and in their careers. This was the first evidence that EQ is a better indicator of success then IQ.

That ability to stop, think and defer gratification is what gives us our humanity. Think about it. When do people get out of alignment with their beliefs and into trouble? If 50 percent of marriages end in divorce, how much of that is driven by one of those people having an affair? In the case of alcohol, drug, or other abuse how much of that is stemming from not being able to defer instant gratification? As a leader, what drives you to do something yourself, versus teaching someone else to do it?

At its base, your EQ really comes down to self-awareness and self-understanding of who you are and what you bring to the table. If you can truly understand what your strengths and weaknesses are, and you're honest and open about them, it will give you a better chance of being successful and finding people to support you.

Personally, if I am aware that I have a need to be needed, and I know that I have low impulse control, if I fall asleep around either of those things, what kind of leader am I going to be?

As Lao Tzu once said, "Knowing others is wisdom, knowing yourself is enlightenment."

ADAPTIVE LEADERSHIP

Being an adaptive leader is about having this constant awareness and working to continuously improve. The question is, how do we keep getting better as the world gets more complex, as the world spins faster, and as technology challenges us?

The key lies in our *adaptability*.

Remember what Lee Thayer, in his book *Leadership: Thinking, Being, Doing* states, "If you want to see the company you deserve, look at the one you have." If you are not professionally or personally getting the outcomes you want, what changes do you have to make?

If you want to change something, what are you doing about it? What is it in your behavior that isn't helping you to get the results you want? Where do you need to adapt, or what do you need to do differently in order to get a different result? Do you have a system in place to get you what you want?

Being an adaptive leader comes back to recognizing your strengths and weaknesses within yourself. Do you have a strong understanding of yourself, your family, or your team? And most importantly, can you talk about it?

Revisiting Susan Scott's *Fierce Conversations*, what fierce conversations aren't you having inside your business or your family? What's the conversation that you need to have with your boss, significant other, spouse, or children?

TIME TO STOP BEING YOUR OWN WORST ENEMY

One of the best ways to stop being your own worst enemy is to work on your EQ to become more effective and fight the urge to fall into comparison traps. Succumbing to the comparison trap really comes down to "I'm not good enough" or "I don't have enough."

If it's about "not having enough," who is that compared to? If you drive a Mercedes and you see a person with a Bentley, you may feel that they have something you don't. Well, what about the Ford owner who's looking at your Mercedes? What about the person who doesn't even have a car? How does that comparison serve anyone?

Now, don't get me wrong, constant improvement and wanting more isn't a bad thing. It can be healthy, as long as you can stop and enjoy what you have and not put a label of "good" or "bad" around what you currently have.

A few years ago, I went on a retreat with one of my groups to the Gauley River in West Virginia. One of the CEOs in my group took five others down with him in his private plane. He was feeling pretty good about himself until a Gulf Stream, a much larger aircraft, taxied up next to his plane, and you could just see him deflate because the Gulf Stream was a bigger toy than he had.

In reality, how many people own private planes? …It's a minute percentage of the population!

I realize better than most that wanting to "do well" is a natural human tendency. Personally, I often fall into this trap by wanting to see my kids do well. The thing that I have to remember is that doing well has to be by their definition, not mine.

At times, when I try and help the kids, and I am out ahead of them, it doesn't serve me or them. If I see them struggling financially or within their relationships, I sometimes just insert myself instead of waiting. I know I have a need to be needed. And in cases like these, I am still learning to exert some impulse control in order to lead from behind, not ahead. Ultimately, when I "trust" my kids to figure things out for themselves we do much better.

BECOMING YOUR OWN ADVOCATE

So, are you ready to become your own advocate? …If so, what does this mean to you? What do you really want? And do you have the self-awareness to know where you might be self-sabotaging or your own worst enemy?

I propose you start by asking yourself the following questions:

- If everything was economically even, what would you choose to do? What makes you feel fulfilled?
- What if when you left the house in the morning, you were really excited to go to work, What does that look like?
- What if, while you were at work, you were really excited to be there? What is the work that excites you?
- What if, while you were driving home from work, you were really looking forward to being with your significant other, spouse, or family? How do you show up in those relationships?

You know as well as I do, most people can't put a success check mark in every aspect of their life. If culture, passion, and EQ are in the right balance to get you what you want, then what else is stopping you, or what's the hurdle you have to overcome to achieve what you want?

Perhaps for you, it's a matter of getting in tune with your strengths and weaknesses and making small adjustments. If so, what can you do to keep your greatest strengths from becoming your greatest weaknesses?

If you are:

- Always drawn to the spotlight. *Spend more time in the shadows.*
- Always in the shadows. *Spend more time in the spotlight.*
- An outgoing "talker" and you think out loud. *Listen more.*
- A great "listener" and all you do is listen. *Do more for yourself.*
- An enabler and people walk all over you. *Confront more.*
- Good at confrontation and assertive. *Be more empathetic.*
- Organized, structured, and sometimes inflexible. *Bring more "messy" into your life.*
- A big-picture thinker. *Pay attention to details.*
- Great at execution and getting things done. *Dream more.*
- A dreamer and a procrastinator. *Keep commitments to yourself and others.*
- Always have the answer. *Ask more questions.*
- Always ask questions. *Make more decisions.*

The biggest growth is counterintuitive. As your own self-advocate, what is your "more"?

CHAPTER NINE
TAKE YOUR ROAD LESS TRAVELED

Take a moment and think back on the actions you've taken in your life. Have you been living a life of accountability and proactive growth? Alternatively, when the going gets tough, do you merely do what you have to do to get by—doing what comes easiest and hoping that external factors will get you to your goal?

Most of us don't change until we hit the proverbial telephone pole. Instead of deferring gratification and taking the harder path to reach higher ground, we get caught in the typical cycle of taking the easy route and end up crashing.

Nike has made a fortune on taking the road less traveled and the slogan "No Pain No Gain." In business school, it's called the "J-Curve."

Accomplishing real change within an organization or our own lives usually requires that we experience some pain and discomfort before we can reap the rewards. As Albert Einstein so astutely observed, "We can't solve problems by using the same kind of thinking we used when we created them."

The concept of the J-Curve goes back to the heart of Marshall Goldsmith's work: *What Got You Here Won't Get You There*. Conceptually, one of the hardest things to learn is that most growth patterns are counterintuitive. As humans, we gravitate to our naturally intuitive behaviors.

WHAT IS THE CURVE OF YOUR JOURNEY?

I think we can all agree that where we are today is where we are. This is our starting point on the J-Curve. As Michelle Saul explains, it's important to get

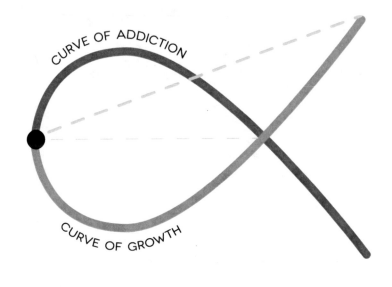

The opposite of the J-Curve is what Michelle Saul refers to as the "Curve of Addiction."

your bearings, much like walking into a shopping center and starting off your shopping excursion by first looking at the site map to locate where you are.

Your starting point on the J-Curve is the reality of today. You know you want to go to a place that's higher up on the curve, to do something that has more meaning, builds more enterprise value, or leads you to more joy. And, like most others, you may like to think that the path that's going to get you there is a dotted line going straight up at a pretty sharp angle. It may be possible to go from your start point to your goal on that growth path, but it will be in incremental steps at best. More often than not, experience tells us this type of growth isn't highly feasible.

The magic behind the J-Curve is that it's all about counterintuitive thinking and *the road less traveled.* As you can see, a typical J-Curve takes a dip down from the start point and then gradually starts climbing back up, ultimately (and hopefully) reaches your end goal and where you want your new starting point to be.

The dip you experience—what I like to call "the cavern"—can be a result of any number of actions you took to reach your end destination. You could have experienced a dip in profits because you invested more in your business, your sales went down, you had a product failure, you hired new people, or you did something that created a short-term negative. When you think of addictive behavior, once a person goes "over the falls," the pain of withdrawal can be brutal. Doesn't it make sense to try and make a change at an easy point, instead of waiting to make the change after the pain gets extreme? Whatever the case might be, you have to stay focused and strong on your ascent out of the cave, to your higher ground.

YOUR CURVE OF ADDICTION

The opposite of the J-Curve is what Michelle Saul refers to as the "Curve of Addiction."

As I mentioned previously, it is human nature to keep doing what we're doing until we crash. If you look at business trends, you will see that people tend to invest at the wrong time and pull back at the wrong time.

Think about what you have heard or read with regard to the stock market or real estate investments. When sales are strong, companies generally bring on additional sales associates and by the time they are trained and productive, the economy enters a slower phase. In the alternative, people tend to cut back on expenses when things get tough and then aren't ready when the market opens up again.

As I discussed before, this also pertains to the sale of businesses. When things are humming and business owners are "winning" and the business has the most market value, they don't sell because they're having too much "fun." Things are good. Traction's at their back and their business is worth a lot of money.

At the bottom, when things are dark, their business is broken, and it's no longer fun, they sell. At this point, they're down at the bottom of the J-Curve and that's when they are forced to sell, typically receiving very little for their business.

How much of their enterprise value do you think they leave behind? However much it is, it's too much!

So, how do you get someone to sell when they're at that top of their bell curve? Especially when they're at the top of their game, the addiction high is feeling good, and it feels like it's going to go on forever?

The United States saw this with the dot-com crash of 2001 and the burst of the housing bubble in 2007. Smart people logically knew the market highs couldn't last, but they couldn't stop themselves. No matter what amount of money they had made on the ride up, they stayed with it. Then it all came crashing down. From a macro point of view, all the fundamentals for market correction were there, but people were addicted to the high.

On a personal level, think back to how many people were well on their way to achieving their retirement goals. Then, after chasing the "new market" in 2007, of subprime mortgages, derivatives and their normal risk-reward relationships, found themselves a long way from fulfilling their needs.

How can you keep from following the downward spiral of addictive behavior in your own personal and professional life? Where are you today?

WHERE THE GREATEST GROWTH HAPPENS

Think back to your greatest times of growth in your life. I am willing to bet that most of you who are reading this experienced your greatest growth as a result of challenging or down times, when something didn't go well. Whether it's losing a job, experiencing a cut in pay, or dealing with a sick family member, this is typically where real growth comes from. I remember, the saddest I had seen my son Michael was when he was cut from his junior high school basketball team, which was the first time he had a negative athletic experience. Doors are truly opened when we are placed in these situations and posed with the challenge of how to pull through. Michael learned and grew from this experience.

On January 26, 2008, a San Diego-based real estate group opened such a door; effectively climbing out of the horrible financial J-Curve, they were in after the housing bubble burst. Transforming a downturn into opportunity, the Coshow Real Estate Group launched the REPO Express, an innovative bus tour that took riders on a guided search for bargains within San Diego County's surging home foreclosure market. Instead of staying within a dried up real estate market that no longer existed, they created another market and not only survived, but profited greatly.

How many people hung on to the real estate business with a death grip, just hoping it would come back? Usually, when I see businesses in trouble, most of the good people are leaving or have already left in search of better opportunities. It's the under performers who stay around because they want someone else to take care of them.

Think back again to the concept of the *Road Less Traveled*. We've all been at that decision point at one time or another. What road do you take? Do you just continue with your current strategy, hoping it will get better? Or, do you take action like one of my Vistage International members at ELKAY, a plumbing, water supply, and cabinet company, who reinvents his business model every three years?

When I was in the shoe business and the domestic sector was in trouble, people would come into my office and ask me, "Bob, can you help me get a job? Can you help me network?"

I would always ask, "Where do you want a job?"

Invariably they would say, "Well, somewhere else in the shoe business."

Baffled, I would respond, "Why? If you visit the local shopping center, where there used to be shoe businesses on the corner, there are now jewelry businesses, or food businesses. Why would you want to stay in a dying business?"

The answer was simple. Instead of being an agent of proactive change and coming to terms with the fact that our skill set isn't around our comfort "known-zone," human nature is typically to give in to addictive behavior.

If there's one thing you can count on, it's that the world economy will continuously be shifting and evolving for as long as you live and beyond. Knowing this certainty, it's important to keep an eye out for the growth industries. What are the skills that you can change, evolve, and move with?

This ability to change and evolve was illustrated in the 2011 movie, *Moneyball*. *Moneyball* told the story of the Oakland A's general manager, Billy Beane, and his successful effort to assemble a baseball team on a lean budget by employing computer-generated analysis to acquire new players. In the age of big business, teams like the New York Yankees and the Los Angeles Dodgers had an advantage because the dollars moving from the stadium to the media gave those teams a financial advantage. By expanding outside of the traditional method of scout-driven player acquisition, the Oakland A's were able to compete in the marketplace against the big corporations and ultimately went on to set the record for the most consecutive wins in a season the following year. We're seeing this approach more and more as small companies that don't have the infrastructure or money to compete ultimately, outperform larger companies because they are faster, quicker, and open-minded to different methodologies.

Authors Renée Mauborgne and W. Chan Kim delved into this concept in their book, *Blue Ocean Strategy: How to Create Uncontested Market Space and Make Competition Irrelevant*. It explored how to get out of the red, shark-infested, competitive ocean, and move into new business possibilities contained in the blue ocean. It is thinking about the non-users of a product and how to convert them. Figuring ways of turning profit out of a customer base that wasn't previously thought about is being an adaptive leader. As mentioned before, Southwest Airlines is committed to making traveling feel like you're on a bus, marketing to a group of customers who don't prefer flying.

An Australian publicly-traded company that employs one of my Vistage International members, recently did something ingenious, embodying this blue ocean approach. They brought him to the United States and made him the President of the Americas. Not the president of North America or U.S., the Americas. Not surprisingly, his biggest growth areas are in Canada and South America. Where many companies would have made him the president of the U.S. business, they were smart enough to recognize the opportunities for expansion in Canada and South and Central America. By focusing in his expertise in the "right places" there were less competitive markets and more rapid growth in revenue, margin, and profits outside the U.S. border.

How many of us put restrictions on our business because we just look at it the way we've always looked at it? I would suggest it's easier to do business in India than it was for our grandparents to do business in Indiana. Although international expansion isn't for everyone, I whole-heartedly believe opportunities should be explored. There are some money managers who feel that the best hedge to an American recession isn't gold, but strong companies with world-wide brands and an expansion of consumer spending around the world.

How do we take that first step down the J-Curve of trial and error, product failure, or new attempts and become open to trying different things?

THE "RISK" OF THINKING ABOUT THINGS DIFFERENTLY

During the boom of the first seven years of this century, risk-takers were, for the most part, financially rewarded. Then, as I briefly mentioned, in 2008 a major correction took place and steadfast "growers" with less tolerance for risk were rewarded. The important point here is that there is no "right" attitude towards risk.

Peter F. Drucker, the well-respected management expert, author, and teacher, probably put it best when he said, "People who DON'T take risks generally make about two big mistakes a year. People who DO take risks generally make about two big mistakes a year."

My father-in-law didn't buy anything he couldn't pay for in cash. For thirty years, I tried to convince Carole that his strategy was flawed. Wouldn't you know, in 2008, his strategy was right on.

Successfully navigating your personal J-Curve really comes down to how you define and think about risk. Remember that example from Orin Harari who drew a tree? There were forty people in suits hugging the core of the tree and one standing out on the thinnest limb. And the caption read, "In today's economy, who is at greater risk?" So, is the risk staying where you are, or is the risk being out on that thinnest branch or somewhere in between?

As I shared previously, authors Warren Bennis and Burt Nanus state: "Managers do things right, leaders do the right thing." If you're defining risk as not being willing to fail then how are you going to succeed into the future? With this mindset, how can you possibly be open to trying new, innovative things?

The same theory applies in your personal life. Are you willing to take some risks, and how do you define risk? How can you transform your business and your life?

As Steven Covey once wrote, "Every organization (*and I would add, your life*) is designed for the output it's getting. If you want a different output, you have to change the organization (*or, again, I would add, your life*)."

Do you want different results? If so, how are you going to think about things differently? How will you change your design?

My "change of design" required me to take two major risks. The first was after we sold Milgram Kagan. I was miserable in the culture there, and, to make it worse, I was bringing it home. Remember, Carole even suspected that I might have been clinically depressed. Making the decision to leave required me to write a six-figure check, not to mention, not knowing where our next source of income would come from. To top it all off, we had two young children at the start of their education and a mortgage to pay. Fortunately, Carole was willing to support me in my "change of design," knowing we would figure it out. And we did.

The second instance took place when my friend Mark's wife had her throat surgery. I still don't know if I approached this the right way, but as Vice President of Milgram Kagan, I took the calculated risk of being with my friend to support him. I could have been fired that day, and I couldn't have argued with the reasons. However, to me, the risk of not being a physical support to my friend was greater.

A personal risk for Carole took place when she told me, five years into our marriage, that she didn't want to be a caretaker anymore and she was going back to school. She even went so far as to share with me, after she was done with her schooling, she wasn't going to be the same person.

This made me realize that sometimes the risk of thinking about things differently has nothing to do with defining your own risk, but in supporting other people's risk and working through it. In this case, Carole was willing to put our marriage at risk because it was the only way she could be the person she wanted to be. She needed to change as a person, to take care of herself, and to start to do some things for herself. To her credit, Carole didn't have to have that conversation with me. However, it was her openness to put it on the table that ultimately worked for us.

Carole would probably say that it scared me. Sure, it was new and I didn't know what it meant, but it enabled us to start thinking about what changes I needed to make in order to make it all work. I can playfully say there were things that I missed. I loved having a caretaker! There are parts I'd still like to have back. That being said, taking that risk and coming out the other side has positively enabled real growth in our relationship and our marriage—growth that continues to this day.

Remember Susan Scott's wise words, "businesses and marriages go bad slowly and then quickly due to the conversations we are unwilling to have."

I have learned to define risk and failure as *not trying*. This learned growth, over time, has helped me build my foundation as a human being. I feel confident in and at peace with who I am. Now, if I put my mind to doing something, I'm not afraid of failure. I'll just keep trying. Remember, "N-O" are just the first two letters of "Not yet."

I would once again ask, what is the curve of your journey? How are you going to "risk" thinking about things differently in your life?

REACHING HIGHER GROUND THROUGH COUNTERINTUITIVENESS

You may be thinking to yourself, "Things are working. Why would I do or think about anything differently?" *Counterintuitive* thinking is what this whole thing is about.

Most examples of counterintuitiveness are of the physical variety. If you're skiing downhill and you start to become unstable, they tell you to lean over your skis towards the downhill slope. If you sit back on your skis, you are probably going to end up on your rear end, or worse. The same counter-intuitiveness applies to driving on the ice. If you hit ice you're supposed to turn into the skid. Sometimes when we get ourselves into trouble, the key to getting out of the predicament is to do the opposite of what we might normally do.

Think about it. If your job is to make your business obsolete before the competition does, that suggests that you need to continue to move yourself and the business forward. It's often about venturing into new markets and trying new things that might feel counterintuitive.

Unfortunately, there's no guarantee that taking your company, or your life for that matter, down the J-Curve will lead to higher ground. As you can imagine, this stops a lot of people. However, I am suggesting that the curve of addiction, although potentially successful in the short term, is a guaranteed, losing proposition for long-term growth.

That's really the purpose of my Vistage International groups—to accelerate the learning of my CEO members. No company can grow faster than its leadership and the higher you go in an organization, the flatter the learning curve.

No company can grow faster than its leadership and the higher you go in an organization, the flatter the learning curve.

SO, WHERE ON THE CURVE OF YOUR JOURNEY ARE YOU?

I was speaking to a group in Minnesota when someone asked me, "How do you know when you've made the journey down the bottom? How do you know when you should stick with what you are doing? How do you know when you are on the up-curve?"

Good questions! How DO you know where you are on the J-Curve?

In his case, his company had embarked upon new product creation, and he was uncertain if he should stick with what they had started or if it was the right time to move on to creating new products.

This is what I shared with him: "If you're the one who started the innovation and now it's in a place where you feel it's getting some traction, and you're starting to move up the J-Curve, it sounds to me like your intuition is telling you to go back to the beginning point in product innovation and start thinking about creating the next product." Intuitively, he had successfully started the business on its J-Curve path. Now, it was time to move on to the next level of innovation.

Instead of falling in love with what you've done, the key is, once you've innovated, to let it fall to other people to execute. It's a continuous cycle of constant improvement. As a result, there could be a lot of J-Curves going on in your life at the same time.

Rafael Pastor, the past Chief Executive Officer of Vistage International, shared a story from when he first became chairman of the board. The late Pat Hyndman, who used to be a Vistage International Chair in San Diego, approached him somewhat aggressively asking him if he was familiar with the system that they used to develop chairs. Rafael indicated that he was, and Hyndman went on to share that he was the individual who created the system. Rafael wasn't sure where this conversation was heading until Hyndman continued to explain that, although he created it, it didn't work anymore, and that Rafael should fix it! How remarkable was that? He was the creator, yet he knew it was time to blow it up and revamp it. The outcome was more important than holding onto something too long.

As David Houle wrote in his book, *The Shift Age*, change is so constant we don't even feel it. In light of this, how can you adapt to change and continue to move your business or family forward?

It's important to remember, all results start with having an ultimate vision.

What is your personal vision for how you want your business, your culture, your family, or your relationships to be? What is your vision for the curve of your journey, you're higher path?

Take a moment to really ponder… Are your business and your life designed to get you what you want? And more importantly, what happens when you get what you want?

Have you ever lusted after a specific car? Sure, the initial journey is exhilarating, but as soon as you leave the parking lot you are now driving a used car. What is your experience and what risks are you willing to take to get a different result?

What would you do differently if you weren't afraid? What are your limiting beliefs? (By the way, they're not true!) What is the result if you don't take any risks and you don't change?

…I would propose that the greater risk is not trying.

CHAPTER TEN

GET IN, GET OUT, GET GOING

Can you imagine a life with significantly less stress?

What if I told you, you could live a life, emptied of stress and filled with joy? Well, I'm here to tell you, you can.

Here's the secret: outside of those who believe that God is involved in everything, what's important is that we view everything in life as neutral. Our interpretations of what happened, through our filters and our experiences, create stress.

As we discussed earlier in this book, we live our lives based off a story that we created in our heads and consistently told ourselves as children. My story was that I wasn't smart enough. This stemmed from my perception of my older brother, Ron, who is fifteen months older than I am. Of course, my story was enhanced by the fact that he also happens to have the exceptional ability of total recall.

Growing up, I begrudgingly followed Ron each year in school. Early on, during our elementary education years, I decided that I could not compete with him academically. Instead I tried to carve out my own identity through sports and being social. And while Ron got "A's," I got detentions.

The experiences of my upbringing only served to cement my personal story of not being good enough or smart enough. If I was playing tennis with my dad and I hit the ball over the net, but I hit it in softly, he would tell me to hit it harder. Now I wasn't just "not good enough," I was "not strong enough" as well. In my mind, whatever I did in life was never good enough for my dad, and therefore, *I wasn't good enough.* As a child, my interpretation wasn't about the "it," it was about "me." My belief is that every child wants their mother's love and their dad's respect.

Eventually, I came to realize my dad and mom did the best they could with the resources they had. I've seen this challenge surface with many people over the years, where they blame their family for their issues, instead of saying, "My parents did the best they could. Am I willing to own my life and to own my decisions? How do I free myself?" What are you going to do? Are you going to be a victim of your family of origin, or are you going to claim your own life?

In an attempt to help me, my parents sent me to boarding school, followed by private school. Nothing changed. I ended up graduating from high school close to last in my class. To seal the conclusion of the story I was telling myself, I never graduated from college.

As I mentioned before, today, I believe I would be labeled with having Attention Deficit Hyperactivity Disorder (ADHD) and medicated. Instead, I was labeled as an "under achiever."

I was living my label. *I was living my five-year-old story.*

During college in the late 1960s, I lost my athlete label when I went to Indiana, a Big 10 University and couldn't compete at that level. I was now a small fish in a big pond at college. I had lost the label that served me, and as far as I was concerned, I had lost my identity.

In my early twenties, my story suddenly changed. In a moment of bravado, I took an IQ test and discovered that I had the same IQ as my brother. Immediately my story shifted to one where I was *smart!*

I still haven't graduated college, yet today I am coaching some of the most successful business leaders and people in the world.

Looking back, I had spent the majority of my academic life in a school system that didn't work for me. Teachers weren't necessarily interested in my curiosity. They were more interested in my compliance. They weren't interested in my uniqueness. What they were interested in, for the most part, was for me to learn how to recite answers and take tests.

Today, when I am working with people and they tell me that their child is having trouble in school, I'll ask, "What is he or she like?" Often, they are creative types and the average school curriculum doesn't allow them to express their "genius." I believe that in a class of 30 students, the established curriculum is usually perfect for student number 15, too slow for the top 14 students and too fast for the bottom 15. Education works best when it is personalized and "genius" is allowed to come forward. With personalization, self-esteem grows and children can develop positive stories, not ones that sabotage them later in life.

> # We put labels on ourselves, our family members and the people in our organizations and then we, and they, live out that label. That is, until we rewrite our adult story.

The story my wife Carole brought into our marriage was "not to trust." At the start, we were quite the pair. I was not smart enough or good enough and Carole didn't trust others. That's not a great recipe for a marriage. I withheld from Carole, so she wouldn't see the real me, and the more that I withheld, the more she had reason not to trust.

As I touched on earlier, Carole was a caretaker. As you can imagine, getting married to a caretaker was a pretty good deal. Yet, it wasn't working for Carole. In review, as a young married couple, because of the personal development work she did, she inspired me to do my own personal work. She also taught me that the only way to intimacy was through vulnerability. That was counterintuitive to how I had "protected" myself my entire life.

Now, do I miss the caretaker? Of course I do sometimes. But our life is much richer because she challenged herself, and ultimately me, to try and get more out of our life together.

Another level of learning arose when I became a Vistage International Chair. As I mentioned previously, I had ventured out to San Diego, California, thinking that I was going to be taught greater facilitation skills by James Newton and Michelle Saul. To my surprise, the actual work was learning and getting in tune with what I was bringing into the room personally. If I was going to do one-on-one coaching with CEOs, then I had to become aware of what my own personal stories, labels, and challenges were. Because I bore the label of not being smart enough, when I tried to prove how smart I was, I usually got in trouble. To the contrary, when I'm able to be my authentic self and be in service to my members, I can be extremely effective.

When you think about that in business and family terms, what's the story that you're telling yourself that's either getting in the way of the productivity of your work or getting in the way of the productivity of your relationships? What's the five-year-old story that has most likely supported you in the past that may no longer be working for you today?

I heard a story about a Vietnamese refugee who, during the Vietnam War, was smuggled out of Vietnam in a fishing boat. He was underneath the tarp as they were crossing the South China Sea, and the fisherman kept referring to him as an orphan. As a result, he wore the label of orphan for a good part of his life. This was the case even after he was a successful businessman and he had a big corner office detached from everyone else in his organization. Obviously, the role of orphan and his fight for a better life contributed to his success in business. However, the big, isolated corner office was sort of a metaphor for his inability to connect with people because he had an orphan mentality. Being an "orphan" protected him for a while, but ultimately, as he grew, he needed to change his story in order to be truly successful in all aspects of his life.

When I'm working with a group of people, I ask them if they want to share, or if they know their story, to please raise their hand. Generally, 50% of the people know their story and they'll raise their hand. The others are usually resistant to share. At a conscious level, about half the people I work with know their story, and it usually falls under the heading of either "I'm not good enough" or "I don't have enough."

The question for all of us is, "What's your five-year-old story that served a purpose at a particular stage in your life?" For me, my labels gave me my identity. But later on in life, not being smart enough and not being able to be intimate in relationships caused me stress and was hindering me from what I really wanted.

So, what's your story, and is it serving you anymore?

THE STRESS OF FILTERS

I recently read the book and saw the HBO movie about the 2008 U.S. presidential elections, *Game Change*, by John Heilemann and Mark Halperin. One of the scenes depicted the moment when Obama won the election. Sarah Palin wanted to go out and make a speech about what a great American John McCain was, and Steve Schmidt, who was the chief advisor of the McCain campaign, told Palin that was not going to happen. In the history of our democracy, what makes our democracy work is that the people have spoken. The losing presidential candidate is the only one who speaks to his supporters, rallying them to unite around the new president and support him as our Commander in Chief. In response, the President stands up and thanks the opposing side and acknowledges the responsibility of becoming the President of the United States of America. It's that compelling moment that signifies that in our democracy, we accept the will of the people and we don't kill each other for change. There's much to be learned from this political process of acceptance and letting go.

Are you aware of how your filters serve you?

A few years ago, I went to interview a candidate for membership into Vistage International, and he had a picture of Ronald Reagan in his office. Curious I asked, "What's the significance of that photo?"

He responded, "Well, he was the greatest president of all time."

Continuing with my line of inquiry I said, "What would it be like for you if you were in a room when people challenged you on that theory? Wouldn't you at least be willing to open to hear why other people might not think that?"

Without budging in his thought process, he once again stated, "No, he was the best president of all time." Ultimately, I didn't want to debate with him whether Reagan was the best president or not because I couldn't prove it one way or the other.

In my estimation, you can still hold your convictions at the end of the day, but you run the risk of stunting your growth and learning. Why is it that so many of us hold on to our convictions to the point of judgment? In reality, the release of judgment is the on-ramp to joy.

Letting go of your filters and embracing curiosity will lead to greater growth and learning. If you want to end a conversation start with "Let me explain why you are wrong," or "You don't understand!" Remember the beach ball? Wouldn't it help to start with, "Help me understand." By the way, I never invited him to join my group.

In another instance, a fellow Vistage International Chair called me to tell me she had brought a member into one of her groups, and the group rebelled against the new member. This person wasn't qualified and, although she admitted she made a mistake, she immediately went on the defensive and went into making excuses. Finally, she asked me, "What would you have said?"

I responded, "Well, if that happened to me, and the group was critical of me for bringing in somebody who didn't fit with the group, I probably would have said. 'You know what, I've been influenced by you guys over these last ten years, watching you bring mediocre people into your company.' Responding like this, a few will laugh at it, and I would make it obvious that I had made a mistake. It doesn't do me any good to defend it. I just need to fix it."

As Carole says to me, "Would you rather be right, or be in a relationship?" If you are trying to convince someone that you are right, doesn't that mean that someone also has to be wrong? You will see, letting go of your need to be right results in more joy.

As Michelle Saul once told me, we're allowed seven nerd-like moments a day, and the greatest joy comes from the ability to laugh at yourself when you have them. (I just try not to use mine up before I leave the house in the morning!) How many people do something that's silly and they beat themselves up all day and all week because of that one moment? …Be a nerd, its okay.

EVERYTHING IN LIFE IS NEUTRAL

I think the first story I ever heard about "everything in life is neutral" was shared by Michelle Saul about two kindergarteners. As she tells it, the two children were walking into kindergarten on the first day of school. As one child goes skipping in, the other is latched onto their mother's ankle. The reality is that they're both embarking on the same general experience. However, one child is going to do it from a fearful place, and one is going to approach it from a place of curiosity and fun.

As I mentioned briefly before, consider Austrian skydiver Felix Baumgartner's jump from a balloon at the edge of the earth's atmosphere, free-falling 128,100 feet and at one point breaking the speed of sound. How do you think he defined risk? My guess is he defined risk as not going. Many of us thought he was absolutely out of his mind.

How is it that some people go skydiving to experience a thrill, whereas some people think its absolute insanity to leave a perfectly good airplane? In another instance, first responders can walk into a building that's on fire because it's the right thing to do. Conversely, how many of us run away from that fire?

In truth, all of these are neutral experiences and then we make our determination. It all comes down to the story you tell yourself. There's no right or wrong, no good or bad, just your interpretation of the data.

RUNNING PROTECTIVE STRATEGIES

Michelle Saul introduced me to a powerful tool called Protective Strategies. The concept is that we run these strategies to cover our insecurities and protect ourselves from being hurt again.

The key is you have to first be aware of what your Protective Strategies are in order to do something about them. In my case, one of my protective strategies is over-explanation. When I get nervous or I don't think I'm good enough or smart enough, I start to over-explain because, in the past, I didn't feel I was heard in my family.

As you can see from the list above, there's a whole list of protective strategies that you can run when your five-year-old self is around. I regularly listen for these when I am facilitating a group. It indicates to me, if someone is being self-righteous, it's really not going to do me much good to have a logical conversation with this person because I'm dealing with a five-year-old.

What protective strategies are you running? Are you projecting a negative outcome? If you are running "self-righteousness," just like that man with the photo of President Reagan, are you open to hearing something different and exploring different possibilities?

Take a few minutes to scan over Michelle's list of Protective Strategies. Pick the one that you think you recognize most in yourself and make that counter strategy visible to others. What other Protective Strategies do you see that other people are running?

12 PROTECTIVE STRATEGIES & COUNTER STRATEGIES BORROWED FROM MICHELLE SAUL'S "POSSIBILITIES" SEMINAR

Strategies we run to cover our insecurities. You have to notice them in order to do something about them.

1. **Self-righteousness:** the need to be right, rationalization, magnification or minimization, "the binocular trick," control, judgment.
   Counter Strategies: openness, humility, listening to others point of view.

2. **Resentment:** blame, bitterness and old buried anger, trying to motivate yourself with shoulds and feeling powerless, feeling like a victim.
   Counter Strategies: own contribution (to event), accountability, forgiveness.

3. **Regret:** shame, guilt over past events or experiences, personalization, burdensome sense of responsibility.
   Counter Strategies: forgiveness (especially of self), gratitude.

4. **Resignation:** giving up, hopelessness, pointlessness, over generalization, seeing a single negative as a never-ending pattern of defeat.
   Counter Strategies: commitment, joy.
5. **Confusion:** refusal to sort information and create a clear picture, difficulty creating closure when making decisions.
   Counter Strategies: clarity, courage, willingness to take a stand.
6. **Worry – Hope:** not present in the moment, go out into the future, construct something negative and focus on it, vision of all reality darkens, fearful, waiting to be rescued.
   Counter Strategies: learning to be in the moment and take action, faith in the future.
7. **Self-Doubt:** lack of belief and trust in self, hesitation, invalidation, arbitrarily concluding that someone is reacting negatively to you and not checking it out.
   Counter Strategies: self-confidence, self-trust, positive self talk.
8. **Explanation:** analytical, always having a reason for everything, avoidance of feelings, fear of being misunderstood or embarrassed.
   Counter Strategies: trust, self-trust, simplicity.
9. **Cynicism:** refusal to join, skepticism, loss of faith and trust in culture, focus on the negative flaw.
   Counter Strategies: learn to join, focus on what's working, faith.
10. **Placation:** giving up a piece of self for the sake of peace, an on-ramp to resentment, fear of conflict.
    Counter Strategies: honest communication, boundaries, learning to say no.
11. **Con:** lack of realness, a wearing of masks, embellishment of truth, looking for short cuts, and the easy way out.
    Counter Strategies: self-awareness, authenticity, hard work, honesty.
12. **Disassociation:** not connected to feelings, checked out, don't even know they're out of touch.
    Counter Strategies: connect to feelings, learn to be present in the moment, self disclosure.

PERSONAL AND ORGANIZATIONAL BURNOUT

In his book, *Wheelspin: The Agile Executive's Manifesto*, Mike Richardson refers to personal and organizational burnout as "wheel spin," or burning out by dealing with the same problem over and over again. The opposite of wheelspin is traction and moving things forward.

I find that my Vistage International groups can fall into this wheelspin trap. If we're not careful, we run the risk of talking about the same problems with the same members all of the time. This ends up sucking the life out of the group because they're not making any progress, and they're not being accountable to making changes. The same thing can happen within a family where they're dealing with the same things over and over again, instead of solving some problems and moving on to a new set of problems.

Generally, when this type of pattern is present, it's an indicator that I'm dealing with an excuse culture, not an accountability culture. In this case, excuses are made as to why things aren't being done: my husband won't support this, the president won't do this, it didn't work last time, we can't do this because _____. (insert excuse)

It's time to stop all of the excuses and step up and be accountable to ourselves and each other! Only then will you be able to take yourself off of the hamster wheel of problems and come up with different solutions.

The movie *Hope Springs*, with Meryl Streep and Tommy Lee Jones, illustrates this concept nicely. After thirty years of marriage, they had just started going through the motions of waking up, sitting down to breakfast, reading the newspaper, and so on. For all intents and purposes, they were stuck in a rut of running the Protective Strategy of *resignation*. Then one day, Kay (Meryl Streep) stepped up and said, "This doesn't work for me anymore. I want something different." They could have gone on with their life, status quo, but neither one of them was being fulfilled. It took one of them, risking everything and trying to create an accountability culture, to ultimately save and grow the relationship.

Another thing that stifles an accountability culture is a concept called "The Peter Principle." The Peter Principle is when people, for one reason or another, are elevated to the level of their incompetence. Once people reach a level of incompetence, they get triggered into protection mode. For example, under the Peter Principle, people are motivated to *protect* their job, rather than to do their job.

I've seen this principle in action with some of the companies I have worked with. In one instance, a CEO made the mistake of promoting a "good sales person" to sales manager, thinking that the person had what it took to be a good manager. This takes us back to the triangle where sometimes it's appropriate to promote from within, but sometimes it's not appropriate to promote from within when we need to bring a certain talent in. However, another challenge arises as soon as we bring in people from the outside and start to push at the culture. It can get messy, but sometimes you have to know when to allow messy and challenge the status quo.

Where are you organizationally and personally? Are you trying to preserve what you've always done, or are you willing to take the risk of trying something new? Or, is the risk really staying where you are?

HOW TO PREVENT PERSONAL AND ORGANIZATIONAL STRESS

A great way you can prevent personal and organizational stress is by introducing something "new." "New" can be a different approach or merely a new perspective and voice at the table.

In the *Harvard Business Review* article I referenced previously, "The CEO's Role in Business Model Reinvention," Vijay Govindaraja and Chris Trimble claimed thirty percent of participants in any strategy discussion should be younger than age thirty, because they are not wedded to the past. Knowing this, are you willing to accept a younger, potentially different way of thinking that challenges your status quo?

When Milton Friedman was interviewed after Hu Jintao, the Premier of China, visited Chicago in 2011 and he was asked if China would become the world power that they "have a right" to be? He responded that if they stay a top-down oligarchy, probably not. However, if they become a bottom-up democracy they have a chance. The problem is that bottom-up democracies are messy.

If you were being honest with yourself, how do you handle "messy?" Are you trying new and different ideas and approaches, or do you merely try and avoid it? Are you just continuing to do the same thing better and constantly looking for improvement?

It's important to remember, managers want to be told what to do. Leaders come up with ideas and then try to get them approved. Remember, it goes back to what Warren Bennis said, "Managers do things right. Leaders do the right thing."

In another article written by Vijay Govindaraja and Chris Trimble for the *Harvard Business Review*, "Building Breakthrough Business within Established Organizations," the authors suggested that people in organizations should be paid for three different things:

1. First, someone should be paid for operational efficiency and profit for the current year.
2. Second, someone should be paid for removing legacy issues and stopping the company from doing things they've always done for the sake of doing them.
3. Thirdly, someone should be paid to fail. Failing was defined as trying new approaches, ideas or products.

When companies are making a lot of money in the present, the tendency is to try to stay with the status quo. However, it's important to realize, although the business might be designed to be efficient today, the efficiencies of today may not be the path to success tomorrow.

If you have a family, natural changes and potential burnout can happen here as well. Where you may want to create friction within a company, it will naturally occur within a family, especially if you have children. This is because families are meant to be dynamic by nature.

Dynamic growth doesn't work when parents try to keep the kids small. I generally see this tension arise when parents try to push back as their kids creatively grow and try new and different things.

I still think the best thing a parent can hear from their friends and family is that they have really great kids. Even though they may look at each other and wonder who these people are talking about because they don't act that way at home, it helps them see through the day-to-day challenges. Kids need to act out and challenge authority on some level. Most importantly, they need to know its okay for them to do it at home. If they're not able to challenge things inside the home, then chances are it will be a more destructive if done outside the family.

Stop and take a moment to think—do you support different, creative, and divergent thinking in your organization and family, or do you push back at it to try and protect the status quo? Do you award your employees or your children for the right things? It is my experience that groups fall into thirds. In a business example- top- adequate- substandard . I think organizations should shine the spotlight on the top bottom influence middle to act the way that they do.

IN SUPPORT OF A MORE JOYOUS LIFE

The number one characteristic or trait that needs to be removed from our lives in order to have a more joyous life is *resentment*. It goes back to the concept that judgment is the onramp to resentment. Release of judgment is the onramp to joy.

Letting go of judgment can be a daunting task. We are all judgmental at times, even myself, but I try to catch it. There is sometimes even good judgment in business and family decisions. But judging others, such as, "we're better" or "we're smarter" is toxic to having more joy in your life.

I said it once, and I'll say it again, the fact is, negative judgment robs us of a more joyous life.

The answer to overcoming judgment and resentment is *awareness*. The problem with judging is that we think we are being judged and we are doing a lot of self-judgment. This is where our five-year-old stories comes back to bite us—I'm not good enough, I'm not smart enough.

PRACTICAL TOOLS TO RELEASE STRESS

When you get stressed, how do you know? Where do you feel it?

In a light-hearted way, I like to play with people by saying, "I'm "fortunate" that my body physiologically lets me know that I'm stressed. I carry most of my stress in my upper back, which is not a vital organ." And so, when I feel a tension in my neck or shoulders, I know I'm under stress.

Others are not so lucky. They feel stress in an increased heart rate, heading possibly to heart disease. Other people suffer from headaches that turn into debilitating migraines or potentially a stroke, while others feel tension in their stomach, and have to deal with colitis and other stress-related stomach disorders.

In their research-driven and yet often humorous book, *Why Zebras Don't Get Ulcers*, Robert M. Sapolsky and Peter Berkrot explain how prolonged stress can cause or intensify a range of physical and mental afflictions. Our nature as human beings, when we worry or experience stress, is for our body to turn on the same physiological responses that an animal's body does. The only problem is that we usually don't turn off our response to stress in the same way—through fight or flight.

Think about the last time you watched a scary movie. As you're watching the movie, you are likely experiencing startling reflexes or other natural reactions. Intellectually, you know you're just reacting to what you're seeing on a screen, but in that moment it feels very real. What this confirms is that our bodies don't know what's real and what's not. We're reacting to our natural tendency of fight or flight.

So, how can you release the stress you experience? I like to share the following five practical tools I learned from Amy K. Hutchinson with my groups, coaching clients, friends, family, and anyone else who will listen:

1. **Just Breathe!** I love this exercise. All you have to do is breathe. By breathing deep, you're signaling to your system that you're not in peril. When you restore your breathing, you should be able to feel your physiology relax, because you are signaling your body that everything is okay. Once I catch my breath and my physiology returns to normal, I try to figure out what's startling or stressful. For me it's usually about, either "I don't have enough" or "I'm not good enough."

2. **Write Down 3 Things.** If I wake up in the middle of the night and I feel tense, it's usually around "I'm not going to have enough money." Once I resolve my physiology and get into a neutral state, I revisit what was making me stressed. I take my worry of "not having enough" and reverse it, visualizing and telling myself that I will have enough money. Lastly, I sit down and write three things that I can do the next day that will ensure the second story is true. It may be that I'll speak to a person that does my investing and make sure we're on the right strategy, I'll look for a little more business, or I'll cut back on my spending.

3. **Everything is Neutral.** If you start to believe the negative story that is causing you stress, the fact is that you will start to live your life in the negative story. Conversely, if you start to believe the positive story, you will start to live your life in line with the positive story and have a better chance for a positive outcome. Remember, it's your choice because everything is neutral.

4. **Blacker's 4 Things.** Neurosurgeon Dr. Martin Blacker outlines four things that you should do to relieve stress: When businesses are under stress or families are going through crisis, we should workout more, eat healthier, sleep better, and do some autogenic training and biofeedback. Under stress, we usually do the exact opposite.

5. **Positively Deal With It!** I would suggest that one of the best ways to deal with stress is dealing directly with the *source* of the stress. Once you identify your source of stress, you can set about removing it and reframing it with positive thoughts and actions. Once you can reframe your source of stress into a positive outcome, focus on it, paint that picture and create action steps towards a positive future.

Taking action, early and often, is KEY. If you think about it, a lot of your stress is probably caused by action that you know you should take and don't.

Taking a positive action will go a long way to remove your stress, personally or organizationally. Take action early and often, while the solution is simple and feasible.

It may just be a matter of having a fierce conversation with ourselves or others. As Susan Scott likes to say, "Businesses and marriages go bad slowly and then quickly due to the conversation we're unwilling to have." It's time to get the conversation started!

What are the actions that you're putting off taking, and why? Are you completely aware of your five-year-old story? This story may have given you some value at some point. Yet, it may now be interfering with your ability to reach your goals and find more joy in your life.

This is what counterintuitive thinking and the J-Curve is all about—this is the road less traveled. Get in, get out, get going!

LIVE YOUR TRUTH, BETWEEN THE SHEETS

Throughout this book, I have shared the fundamentals that I utilize with my clients and practice in my own life—both personally and professionally. Perhaps you connected to some of what I shared intellectually, or in some cases (I hope) you also connected to what I've shared on an emotional level. If you have, I encourage you to allow yourself to feel the emotions you are experiencing. Only then will you be able to truly shift your current behaviors and choices to ones that support less stress and more joy in your life.

Before you set this book down, take a moment to revisit a few of the key concepts of leadership I've shared. Where do you currently fit into each? Most importantly, are the actions you're taking, and the life you're living, truly serving you?

LEADERSHIP CONCEPT 1: VISIONARY LEADERSHIP

All of the insights I've shared have revolved around what it means to be a leader, not a manager. As I like to remind my coaching clients to help keep them on track, "Managers do things right, whereas *leaders do the right thing.*"

Be honest with yourself. Are you currently a leader or are you a manager? Going back to one of the first questions I posed to you, what are your *ingoaltions*—the intentions and goals you've set out for yourself? What is your vision and how are you going to get there? Are there gaps? If yes, what are your counterintuitive moves that will move you closer to the outcome that you want?

As the 35th president of the United States, John F. Kennedy had what Jim Collins calls a *big hairy audacious goal.* He had a vision to take a man to the moon and bring him back. I believe that President Kennedy had no earthly idea how to accomplish this. However, what he did to was set out a clear vision so that everyone at NASA knew what their part was in accomplishing this monumental feat. The clear directive was to build a rocket that could safely get a man to the moon and back. This vision clearly set the standard for development of the communication systems all the way down to the proper amount of food needed to last the duration of the mission.

If you look at successful leaders, most of them had a big hairy audacious goal and a vision to get there. In 1935, President Roosevelt signed an executive order creating the Rural Electrification Administration and started the ball rolling to establish electricity in every home, in every corner of the United States. Similarly, President Dwight D. Eisenhower presented the United States with the "Grand Plan" in 1954, effectively instigating the creation of a system of interstate highways throughout the country.

In every instance, the business solutions and practical execution can be tied back to the strategic vision of the leader. Without this strategic vision, even the best-laid plans will fall apart. Remember the work I referenced earlier by anthropologists who studied trekking in the Himalayas? They discovered that groups stayed together during their treks in the Himalaya's and discipline only broke apart at the very end when they were descending on the last leg of their trek. The reason they broke apart on the way back to base camp is because they no longer had a compelling saga or vision ahead of them. Without a compelling vision, people fill in this void on their own and it's rarely constructive to the vision of the business or the unity of the family.

This concept of visionary leadership is just as applicable to your personal life, as it is to your business life. How many parents tell their children, "Study [insert profession of your choice], because these are the jobs that are available today." Isn't this really serving you? Instead, shouldn't you be thinking of and setting the vision for the opportunities in the world that they are going to be living in, and not the world that *you* live in?

Visionary leadership is about having big hairy audacious goals, big picture thinking, and even, yes, you guessed it, *ingoaltions.* There are many examples of visionary leadership surrounding us every day. They are the examples like you read about regarding Walgreen's, where the president of Walgreen's saw the imminent market shift that nobody else saw. It's represented in that article in *The Wall Street Journal* in 2000, where it suggested that picking the next president wasn't about Mr. Gore or Mr. Bush personally, it was about *who do you think has the best chance to see around the corner.*

Now I would ask you to consider, where and how is your visionary leadership going to show itself? What would you do if you weren't afraid? How are you defining risk?

LEADERSHIP CONCEPT 2: EXECUTION

As I've frequently referenced throughout this book, the foundational bodies of work that best support this concept of execution are Susan Scott's *Fierce Conversations* and Patrick Lencioni's *The Five Dysfunctions of a Team.*

One of Susan's premises in the book is: "Businesses and marriages go bad slowly, then quickly, due to the conversations that we're unwilling to have." So my question to you is, Are there any conversations that you've been unwilling to have within your family, your friendships, or your organization? Historically, when we delay those conversations, the issues we're dealing with are much worse than if we cut them off in the beginning. It's time to start talking!

Another key aspect to execution, which Lencioni addresses in *The Five Dysfunctions of a Team*, is after we have violated someone's trust, how do we rebuild it? There are three fundamental levels of trust to always be mindful of:

- Level One: Do I lie, do I steal?
- Level Two: Am I willing to do what I said I would do, when I said I would do it, period?
- Level Three, the highest level of trust: Am I willing to speak my truth? Do I trust myself enough and do I trust our relationship enough where I can speak my truth?

LEADERSHIP CONCEPT 3: STAYING CURIOUS

When I am working with leaders, and people in general, I often ask them to stay curious. Again, revisiting Susan Scott's beach ball, if I'm on the top of it and its green, there's no doubt that my world is green. If somebody's on the other side of the beach ball and they see blue, there's no doubt that they have a blue worldview. Similarly, in a functional organization or family, we're staying curious as to why people see things differently than we do. In a dysfunctional organization or family, we try to convince everybody that we're right. In my experience, being right is overrated. Think about it, would you rather be right, or would you rather be in a successful business or personal relationship?

From a political standpoint, we see this concept arise on a regular basis. When Democrats or Republicans try to convince the opposing party that their view of the world is incorrect, it's dysfunctional. Instead, they would better serve themselves, and their party, by just staying curious about how the other party sees things differently.

Organizationally, it's not unusual for people to be resistant to individuals who are catalysts for change. A key to successful leadership lays in the willingness to be curious about other people's views and interpretations. It's important to always stay open to new ideas and learning.

The name of the game is focusing on what makes your company or family great. As a leader, that great idea or vision is what you should be managing down to the detail level. Remember, in order to grow an organization, you have to be comfortable with some things being broken, just not the wrong things.

Revisiting Susan Scott's "Decision Tree," keeping in mind the following issues will help you to delegate decision-making more effectively and efficiently:

- **Leaf Issues** should be able to be decided by anyone in the organization.
- **Branch Issues** should be able to be decided by anyone in the organization but checked one level up before executed.
- **Trunk Issues** can impact many different pieces of the organization and decisions should be brought to the senior leadership table.
- **Root Issues** are the decisions that only senior leadership should make, as they could ultimately destroy or help the tree prosper.

It's not unusual to experience resistance when someone with a new way of thinking is brought in from outside the organization. In many cases, people within the company many even try to sabotage that new thinking. As counterintuitive as it may seem, from friction, comes growth.

How many people are comfortable enough in their leadership to honor that friction? As a leader, are you willing to allow that friction to take place?

THE LARGER LESSON—CHECKING-IN
TO ALL ASPECTS OF LEADERSHIP AND YOUR LIFE

So, what does it really mean to lead a life of leadership? As author Simon Sinek likes to share, being a leader is simple—you merely need to have followers!

All quipping aside, leading a life of leadership doesn't have to be complicated. The single biggest waste of time on the planet is wishing for a better past. All you can do in the present is move forward and take steps to preserve and enhance life. Your future set of actions is the only solution.

In your life, you have two families, your personal family and your organizational family. As I recently heard Simon Senik explain, "Stop saying, 'our company is like a family.' You are the mother and you are the father. The minute you hire someone you must give them undying love, you must work tirelessly to make sure they can achieve more than you could have ever imagined yourself achieving. *Those are the best leaders.* That's what it means to be a *servant leader.*"

Take a moment to really think about this. As a leader, what is your responsibility to:

- Your **family**?
- Your **organization**?
- Your **industry**?
- Your **community**?

As Lee Thayer once said, "If you want to see the life you deserve, look at what you've got." So, what kind of life do you have?

People often ask me, "Why are you doing this?" Well, it's because I was lucky enough to get 'hit up side the head' when I was fifty!

This is not about "training," it's about personal development. I've had to make the hard decisions and embrace change in my own life. I've walked away from a business and had to write a six-figure check, not knowing where my income was coming from. Carole challenged us to seek "more" and get more out of our relationship and our lives. None of this was easy, but the gains in life have been well worth it. I've explored my own personal unknowns and consistently try to move beyond my comfort zone.

My own personal growth did not come without role models. I'm grateful that I had two grandfathers that shared their two models of success with me, just by living their lives.

Both my grandfathers ran successful businesses. Grandpa Harry lived on Park Avenue in New York City. He drove nice cars, took nice vacations, and ate at fine restaurants. He wanted his customers to see him as successful. His belief was, people wanted to be around success.

On the opposite end of the spectrum, my other grandfather, Grandpa

Dave, lived in a two flat walk-up in Brooklyn, owned an accounting firm, and drove a 1955 Buick until the wheels fell off. Counter to my other grandfather's lifestyle, he lived a very moderate, charitable life. He didn't have a lot of creature needs and his story was, "I didn't want my customers to think I was charging them too much."

Throughout his adult life, my Grandpa Dave was very generous to his Temple. If someone at the Temple needed money for a bar mitzvah, or for a life-cycle event, my grandfather was the go-to guy. But my grandfather never forgot who he helped. Over the years, he would watch each and every person he was charitable to. If they grew into successful careers, he went and knocked on their doors and told them it was time to give back to those who were now in need.

At one point, the Temple wanted to honor him and he wouldn't accept that adoration. They were finally able convince him to allow them to honor him by establishing a foundation that helped others in the community. And so, I was brought up as a young child, watching my grandfather give away whatever excess profit he received, what I like to call "goodies," as fast as he could.

As a result of my Grandpa Dave, I became very involved in foundation work, mostly in Jewish charities. When both of my children married wonderful people outside of the Jewish faith, in honor of their lifestyle, I started to look to see where I could broaden my charitable giving to more social nonreligious organizations.

In 2010, the birth of third grandchild, Brayden, provided a new direction for the entire family. You see, Brayden was born with a faulty heart valve. Although we were fortunate to get the best medical care for him, we also saw this as an opportunity to help others in need. So, I put my business skills and my ability to connect with other people with capital to work.

What could have been viewed solely as a family crisis transformed itself into an opportunity for the entire family to give back to others for a lifetime. In 2011, as a family, we launched *A Giving Heart Foundation*, dedicated to saving the lives of children with congenital heart disease. With two generations of family on the foundation Board, I can't help but feel what an amazing gift it has been to work with my children and their spouses towards a common good. Not only have we been able to take care of our own Brayden, but at the same time, heal other children in the world with congenital heart defects.

So that's one of my new stories of being *good enough* and *having enough*. Although Brayden was unfortunately born with a faulty heart valve, he has provided me with the gift of allowing me to connect my three pillars of happiness—loving what I do, being in service, and being around kids.

As Joseph Campbell so astutely observed, "Opportunities to find deeper powers within ourselves come when life seems most challenging."

I've lived the J-Curve. I'm not asking you, or anyone else to do anything I haven't done myself. I've gone through that valley of the J-Curve and thankfully can now report what it looks like from the other side. And I've also been there with numerous others as they've gone through that valley and come up the other side.

That's what I wish for you—the best, whatever that means for you. I was fortunate to grow up observing two different models of success. So, as you can see, there isn't just one way or just one path. Most importantly, it's not about being right. It's about what works for you.

YOU'RE IN 'CHOICE' EVERY MINUTE OF EVERY DAY

It goes back to what Coach Weinhauer shared with us in that high school gym locker room all those years ago, "What I had I gave, what I kept is lost forever." You're either playing "all-in," being 100% in the moment, or you're not. It's as simple as that.

You're in "choice" every minute of every day, and the choices that you make have an impact on your life and those in your personal and organizational families. Coach Weinauer had that influence on me. In a similar way, it was eye-opening to me for Scott Rude to stand up at Ditka's Restaurant before Michael's wedding to share the impact I had on him by just challenging him to have a goal.

As Steve Jobs said at his speech at Stanford in 2005, "You can't connect the dots looking forward; you can only connect them looking backwards. So you have to trust that the dots will somehow connect in your future. You have to trust in something — your gut, destiny, life, good karma, whatever. This approach has never let me down, and it has made all the difference in my life."

Changing your beliefs changes your behaviors, while changing your behaviors will change your results. Choose to have less stress and more joy in your life. You are good enough and you do have enough. It's time to shed yourself of your old story that isn't serving you anymore.

What's your new story?

Freed of your old script, get busy living all-in and share this with your children and others. Show up authentically and deepen your own realizations and learnings, by teaching these concepts to others and leading by example. … Start living your truth, between the sheets.

F-TEST

Don't turn the page over until you read to the end of this paragraph. At the end of this paragraph, turn the page and read what is written on the opposite page, and when you're done, turn the page back to this page.

Now that you have read through what is on the next page, do it again. This time read what is written, without touching the page, and count how many F's you see. When you're done turn the page back over. Now, write down how many F's you saw in the paragraph. After you're finished, turn back to Chapter 4 to read more about the F-test.

FINISHED FILES ARE THE
RESULT OF YEARS OF
SCIENTIFIC STUDY COMBINED
WITH THE EXPERIENCE OF
MANY YEARS OF EXPERTS